Fire Precautions in Computer Installations

M B Wood

PUBLISHED BY NCC PUBLICATIONS

[redacted]

British Library Cataloguing in Publication Data

Wood, Michael B.
Fire precautions in computer installations.
1. Electronic data processing departments – fires and fire prevention.
I. Title
628.9'22 TH9445.E45

ISBN 0-85012-556-1

First published in 1986 by:

NCC Publications, The National Computing Centre Limited, Oxford Road, Manchester M1 7ED, England.

Typeset in 11pt Times Roman by Manntype Typesetting Specialists, Fourways House, 18 Tariff Street, Manchester M1 2EP; and printed by Hobbs the Printers of Southampton.

ISBN 0-85012-556-1

Preface

Fire is a serious threat for any organisation, and the losses from fire are increasing. The British Insurance Association reported that in the first eleven months of 1984 fire caused damage of £506.8 million. The consequential losses probably cost the country at least as much again.

Information technology (IT) is increasingly important throughout commerce and public administration. Fire protection of the equipment and data needed to support essential information systems is often weak. Many organisations install small computers and office systems in ordinary offices and other buildings that were not designed to house electronic systems, with their associated power supplies and cabling. Elementary fire precautions are often missing, and modern fire engineering knowledge is ignored, even in otherwise well-conducted installations. Fire protection legislation is intended mainly to protect life and limb, not the vital information systems, although standards do exist for large computer installations.

A revised version of the relevant British Standard code of practice was issued in 1982. New materials pose unexpected fire threats, and IT installations are particularly vulnerable to damage by smoke and fumes. Radical thinking is needed if the industry is to escape the consequences of an increasing burden of fire loss.

This book is not a definitive guide. The intention is to draw attention to the existing body of fire engineering knowledge and experience, and relate it to computer centres and other applications of information technology. The report concentrates on practice in the United

Kingdom. Circumstances vary from one country to another, so that a universal prescription is not possible; overseas readers should take account of legislation and practice in their own countries.

Every computer installation is different. The measures that are appropriate in one installation will not necessarily be right in another. In each individual case the risks from fire must be assessed. Nonetheless, guidelines and basic precautions can be given. Appropriate measures can then be adopted to meet local circumstances.

Acknowledgements

This book draws upon the published work of many experts in fire engineering and computer security. The book could not have been produced without this established body of knowledge. Some of the sources used are listed at the end of the book under Further Reading.

Several people very kindly read the draft, and made valuable comments and suggestions. My thanks go to Mr G W C Hayes (TSB England and Wales), Mr D T Lindsay (Philips Electronics ISA-UK), Mr J M Riggs (British Airways), Mr G Vallance (Unipart Group Ltd), and to colleagues Mr W G Berry and Mr B Chapman at NCC. Special thanks also go to my wife Rosemary, who read several drafts.

Contents

1 Introduction

THE THREAT OF FIRE

Fire is arguably one of the most serious threats faced by any organisation. The losses from fire increase year by year. The British Insurance Association reported that, in the first eleven months of 1984, fire caused damage of £506.8 million in the UK. The Fire Protection Association estimated the loss for the year at £553.6 million. It reported that there were 979 large fires costing £50,000 or more, accounting for 73 per cent of the estimated damage. During November 1984 alone, there were five fires that cost more than £1 million each.

Fire losses have low probability, but may have very high severity. Computers and computer installations are especially vulnerable to damage by fire. The computer equipment and its associated magnetic media – disks and tapes – are easily damaged by heat. They can be ruined by the slightest contamination with smoke, perhaps from a fire in a nearby area. The material damage that results from even a small fire in or near a computer room can be very great indeed.

Fire generates heat, smoke and toxic fumes. If it is not quickly brought under control, even a small fire can spread rapidly throughout a building. Fire may spread up a stairway, or a lift shaft. If there is a plentiful supply of combustible material the fire may burst through the windows and ignite the floor above. A computer centre may be affected by a fire elsewhere in the premises, especially if lack of proper fire separation in the construction allows the centre to be contaminated by smoke or fumes.

At a bank in London, in October 1978, an air conditioning unit in the computer centre caught fire. Smoke detectors gave the alarm, and the fire was quickly extinguished, but not before the fans had dispersed smoke into the computer room. A brand new ICL mainframe was being commissioned, but became a total loss following the contamination. The loss was more than £1.3 million.

If the fire should result in the loss of vital records or data, the consequences for the organisation can be very grave. Another point that must be considered is the loss of processing capability that can result from a fire. These indirect or consequential losses following a fire can be far greater than the material damage caused by the actual blaze.

Consequential losses usually exceed direct material damage losses. A study (reported by Schroeder, 1985) of 100 ordinary big claims from industrial companies around the world with good insurance records showed that the average insured direct loss was $2.51 million. The average insured consequential loss amounted to $3.03 million. The uninsured business losses are not known, but could include such items as:

- loss of market share, clients and customers;
- loss of previous investments made in marketing, research and development which are worthless when products cannot be delivered;
- loss of important documents;
- damage to corporate image;
- loss of revenue from new products that cannot be introduced as planned;
- loss of productive time spent in investigations and legal actions;
- loss of favourable conditions, such as good purchasing contracts, or favourable building codes.

Many smaller organisations have inadequate consequential loss insurance, and often only have cover for increased costs for as little as twelve months after a contingency.

A serious major fire in nearby premises can result in denial of access to a computer facility that may itself be quite undamaged. The senior fire officer at an incident has wide powers; in serious incidents access to the site might be denied for several days, which could be very damaging for the organisation. The fire threats in the neighbourhood, as well as those within the immediate computer area and its surroundings, should be assessed.

Above all, one must remember that even a small fire is a most serious hazard to people. Fire and smoke can cause serious permanent injury or even death. Everyone concerned must ensure that appropriate precautions are in place and that proper procedures are always followed to minimise the risk of a fire occurring in or near the computer installation. This demands constant attention to the education and training of all staff, and the vigilant monitoring of circumstances.

Fires still happen even where the best precautions have been taken to prevent them. The precautions should therefore also attempt to minimise the consequences if a fire should occur.

Early detection is vital. The first few minutes of a fire are critical. Automatic detectors should be used, even for small installations. Here, shift working is now unusual. Ordinary office hours are increasingly common. As a result, the premises may be unoccupied for about three-quarters of the 168 hours in a week.

FIRE PRECAUTIONS

Fire precautions are defined in *BS 4422 : Glossary of Terms associated with Fire* as "the measures taken and the fire protection provided in a building or other fire risk to minimise the risk to the occupants, contents and structure from outbreak of fire".

Fire precautions can be divided into two parts: fire prevention and fire protection. Obviously every effort should be made to prevent fires from starting in the first place. Fire prevention aims to do this. However, if a fire should start, appropriate fire protection measures will minimise its severity and likely consequences. Fire protection in turn has two components: passive fire protection and active fire protection.

Passive fire protection includes structural fire protection and provision of adequate means for escape. The furniture and fittings in a building may have a major impact on the behaviour of any fire that does break out. A wise selection, taking account of the fire properties of the materials, may pay big dividends. Passive fire protection is covered in Chapters 3 to 7 which deal with the building, its services, and its contents (including vital records).

In one sense the fire precautions have failed if fire does break out. For this reason, this book concentrates first on fire prevention and passive fire protection, leaving active fire precautions to later chapters.

Active fire protection comes into its own if fire should break out. It includes fire detection and fire quenching, which are discussed in Chapters 8 and 9.

Fire protection demands constant vigilance from everyone involved in an enterprise. There must be proper training and instruction in fire protection. The action to be taken in case of fire must be established, with proper allocation of responsibility. Determined and disciplined attitudes are necessary in relation to housekeeping, and general tidiness within the computer environment. Operational aspects are discussed in Chapter 10.

Chapter 11 brings together many of the points made in other chapters as a series of guidelines. Each individual installation can use those that are appropriate.

Lists of useful addresses and further reading complete the book.

LEGISLATION

Many countries have fire-protection laws designed to ensure adherence to at least minimum standards. Most legislation is designed primarily to safeguard life, rather than to protect property.

Fire-precautions legislation in the United Kingdom is very complex, and only an outline can be given here. The main items of legislation that apply to offices and computer centres are:

> The relevant Acts and Regulations for new buildings, extensions and alterations (which cover structural fire protection measures);
>
> The Fire Precautions Act 1971;

The Health and Safety at Work, etc Act 1974, which, besides imposing duties on all those involved in the work situation, amended the 1971 Act;

The Fire Precautions Act 1971 (Modifications) Regulations 1976 (SI No 2007).

Many other statutes and regulations are concerned with particular aspects of fire precautions. The situation varies for different kinds of premises and industries, especially those using hazardous processes or materials.

The basic aim of the building regulations, in control of structural fire protection, is to ensure that the building structure is not unduly hazardous in the event of fire, and that it will ensure (within reasonable limits) the safety of all persons who might become involved. Any new buildings and extensions (including alterations) will need to comply with the appropriate building regulations. The UK has four different sets. There are separate regulations for England and Wales, excluding Inner London; Inner London (the thirteen London Boroughs covering the old LCC area); Scotland; and Northern Ireland.

The Fire Precautions Act 1971 provides powers in relation to almost all kinds of premises. Offices, Shops and Factories have been designated under the Act. Much of the earlier legislation has been superseded by the Act. Guides have been issued by the Home Office.

Occupied premises, unless exempted, may require a Fire Certificate from the Fire Authority. The Fire Certificate specifies details of the fire precautions in use, and the uses of the premises which are covered by the certificate. The fire precautions will include provision of means for escape in case of fire, structural protection of escape routes, the fire warning system, and the means of fire fighting available. The Act is far-reaching. It requires that the Fire Authority must be informed if it is proposed to make any material extension of, or material structural alteration to, the premises; or to make a material alteration in the internal arrangement of the certificated premises or in the furniture or equipment with which the premises are provided.

The Home Office Guides explain that "material" means any alteration that would render the means of escape and related fire precautions inadequate in relation to the normal conditions of use of the premises at the time the fire certificate was issued. If in doubt, it is wisest to consult the fire authority before making any changes, even if these are only temporary.

It is an offence to make such change without having given notice of the proposal to the fire authority. The penalty on summary conviction is a fine not exceeding level 5 on the standard scale, and, on conviction on indictment, a fine or imprisonment for a term not exceeding 2 years, or both.

SOURCES OF INFORMATION

(Addresses and other details are listed at the end of the book.)

The Home Office *Guides to the Fire Precautions Act 1971. Number 3. Offices, Shops and Railway Premises* is essential reading. It includes a guide to the Act, and a guide to fire precautions.

There is an excellent discussion of the Act in a collection of papers called *The Fire Precautions Act in Practice* edited by Jane Taylor and Gordon Cooke.

Several books in the Home Office *Manual of Firemanship* can be recommended. *Book 8, Building Construction and Structural Fire Protection,* covers materials, elements of structure and building design. *Book 9, Fire Protection of Buildings,* includes clear descriptions of the various fire extinguishing systems, fire alarm systems, and fire venting systems. *Book 10, Fire Brigade Communication,* provides an insight into the call-out and mobilising systems used by the brigades, and automatic fire alarm signalling systems. The local fire authority and the fire insurers should be consulted at an early stage during planning of the installation or consideration of any changes to its layout or construction.

The Fire Protection Association is a major source of information. It has an extensive publications list, and produces a *Compendium of Fire Safety Data,* a collection of more than 245 data sheets on all aspects of fire, its prevention and control. The FPA has available several films and videos, and collections of slides that can be used in training. It also runs courses and organises seminars.

The fire authorities, insurance companies and the FPA have set up a regional fire safety organisation under the Central Fire Liaison Panel.

There is a nationwide system of Fire Liaison Panels, whose addresses can be obtained from the central secretariat of the FPA. The Panels organise local conferences where ideas for fire safety are exchanged. The Industrial Fire Protection Association, and many local fire protection associations, also actively promote fire safety.

The Greater London Council's very clear *Code of Practice: Means of Escape in Case of Fire* can be recommended.

Insurance companies are very concerned about fire losses because of their high potential cost. In the course of insuring others against fire risks, the companies have accumulated a vast amount of experience about fires in buildings. More recently the experience includes fires in computer installations, and similar concentrations of valuable electronic equipment such as the modern electronic telephone exchange. The fire insurers are represented by the Fire Offices' Committee, often abbreviated to FOC. (This represents the insurers, not the fire officers, of the Fire Authorities.)

The Fire Offices' Committee and the Fire Offices' Committee of Ireland issue *Recommendations for the Protection of Computer Installations Against Fire.* This includes recommendations about the construction of the computer area, about protection of equipment and space, floor and ceiling voids, about air conditioning, and the protection of records. The original edition, issued in December 1979, was revised in 1985. The FOC has also issued *Rules for Automatic Fire Alarm Installations.* The original issue, published in June 1983, has now been revised.

In the United Kingdom most installations will have ready access to the expert knowledge of the local fire service. It is an advantage if the fire brigade is familiar with the layout of the installation. It is possible that at some time they may have to fight a fire whilst hindered by dense smoke. A fire officer who knows the building and its layout will be better placed to fight the fire. The fire officer will be able to offer useful advice.

There is a British Standard code of practice for *Fire Protection for Electronic Data Processing Installations*. BS 6266: 1982. This is a revision of CP 95: 1970. It offers specific guidance about all aspects of the installation, including: accommodation; air conditioning; power distribution including alternative supplies; and fire detection and extinction. It goes further than the FOC Recommendations by giving guidance on operational aspects of fire protection. It discusses topics such as training, the protection of records, and the action to be taken before staff leave the premises after working hours.

Another useful source is section 2.5 of the *Management Handbook of Computer Security* (Waring) published by NCC.

The US Department of Commerce has issued a *Standard Practice for the Fire Protection of Essential Electronic Equipment Operations.* Prepared by the National Fire Prevention and Control Administration, this is a most practical guide to fire protection thinking. It contains detailed case histories of many actual fires in computers, radar installations, electronic exchanges, etc. The detailed recommendations should be treated with caution by readers outside the United States because different standards may well apply.

There are many other relevant sources of information on fire precautions. The national standards bodies, such as BSI, issue many relevant specifications and codes of practice. The insurers issue lists of approved appliances, manufacturers, suppliers and installers. There are fire testing standards for building materials and construction, for electric cables, and for other items like fire data safes.

The Fire Research Station at Borehamwood, Hertfordshire, was established in 1947 and undertakes research into all aspects of fire. It has an extensive publications list, and one of the largest libraries in the world on the subject of fire. It also has an advisory service to deal with problems related to fire.

The Insurance Technical Bureau, among other things, has special interest and expertise in safeguarding electronic equipment from corrosion following a fire. Here prompt special cleaning is recommended.

The Fire Insurers' Research and Testing Organisation (FIRTO) is concerned with the testing of fire protection equipment, such as fire detectors, sprinkler systems, and halon and carbon dioxide systems. It also conducts fire tests to BS 476 for elements of building construction.

The major computer manufacturers can offer specific advice about their own equipment. User group meetings sometimes discuss fire protection and disaster planning.

Some idea of the variety of fire protection equipment that is available is given by the annual catalogue *FITECH International*. A comprehensive UK directory is *Security and Fire Protection Yearbook* which gives addresses and details for all kinds of organisations and authorities.

Much equipment is displayed at the annual International Fire, Safety and Security Exhibition (IFSSEC) held in April each year at London's Olympia, and organised by Victor Green Publications. The FPA and its Fire Service partners within the Federation of British Fire Organisations organised Fire International '84, with a major conference and full international exhibition of equipment. Events have been booked for Eastbourne (1985), Glasgow (1986), Bristol (1987), London (1988) and the next full international event in Birmingham (1989).

Several specialist journals carry occasional articles relevant to fire precautions in computer installations. They include, for instance: *Fire Prevention; Fire International; Fire Surveyor; Risk and Loss Management; Health and Safety at Work; International Security Review; Security and Protection; Security Gazette; and Security World.* Other journals carry accounts of actual fires that have affected computer installations. Often these accounts explain how the organisation recovered from the disaster. They provide much food for thought.

2 Understanding Fire

THE THREE ESSENTIALS

Fire needs three things if it is to persist – heat, fuel and oxygen. This is often called the fire triangle. The threat of fire can be reduced by eliminating one or more of the three components. If there are no combustible materials there is no fuel to feed the fire. A fire can be quenched if it can be cooled sufficiently, thus removing the heat that is necessary to sustain combustion. This happens when a fire is extinguished by dousing it with plenty of cold water. The supply of air to a fire provides the necessary oxygen for combustion. Deny it air and the fire will die. This can be done with a fire blanket, or by flooding the area with a gas like carbon dioxide.

BEHAVIOUR OF FIRE

Unfortunately for theorists, fire does not behave predictably. Staff in fire research laboratories often have great difficulty in producing repeatable fires for experimental purposes. Anyone with experience of lighting a domestic open fire, or getting an open-air barbecue to work effectively, will appreciate some of the problems.

Fortunately for fire protection, most materials do not ignite very readily. Those that are easily ignited are used as tinder when one wants to start a fire. A combustible material will start burning if its temperature is raised sufficiently by some external source of heat. Burning is a complex set of chemical reactions in which the burning substances combine with oxygen to produce heat and light. Once a substance is ignited the burning reaction may generate enough heat to ignite the surrounding material. If this happens the substance will continue to burn. The fire will grow in size until it reaches the limits of the available fuel or oxygen supplies.

Other materials are difficult to ignite. They will burn if there is a plentiful supply of heat, but their own combustion does not produce enough to sustain the reaction. Many other materials resist burning even at high temperatures.

Oxygen is needed if combustion is to occur. An atmosphere enriched with oxygen facilitates burning. Materials will burn more easily in air that is enriched with oxygen, so that supplies of the gas constitute a special fire hazard.

The structure of a material affects its fire performance. Thin films, gauzes and fine powders often burn much more readily than does the same substance in the solid. Magnesium ribbon can be ignited with a match, but a large block of magnesium conducts heat away so rapidly that it is difficult to ignite. Powders dispersed in air often form explosive mixtures, partly because the surface area of each particle is very great in relation to its tiny mass, so that a plentiful supply of oxygen is available to support explosive burning.

Combinations of two or more materials often behave quite differently from the separate materials. For example, it is difficult to ignite a piece of candle wax using a match, but with a suitable wick one can light the candle quite easily. The fire properties of a combination are often not so easy to predict. This unpredictable behaviour of combinations is an important factor in selecting materials for interior finishes and furnishings. One should demand fire test information before making a choice.

DEVELOPMENT OF ROOM FIRE

A fire in a compartment such as a room can be divided into three phases; growth, steady state and decay. In the growth stage the materials will be ignited, usually from a small source. If there is sufficient feedback of generated heat the fire will grow, assuming that combustible materials are at hand. Fortunately most fires do not progress beyond this stage. They either decay quickly for lack of suitable fuel nearby or there is inadequate feedback of heat. Fires are often discovered before they progress too far, especially if someone smells burning.

Electrical fittings sometimes overheat because of a loose

connection. The insulation breaks down, and may "track", often producing a fishy smell, which may be overlooked for several days. All unusual smells should be thoroughly investigated, because they are often an early indication of material that is overheating.

Sometimes the fire takes hold, and quickly grows in size and ferocity, consuming more and more fuel, faster and faster, until its growth is checked in some way. The size of the fire may be limited by the available fuel, or the amount of ventilation, or by the configuration of the room and its contents.

The second stage is reached when growth is limited. Steady-state combustion follows, and the size of the fire is limited by some factor that prevents further growth. As it burns the fire may break out and secure extra fuel or air, possibly with dramatic consequences. It is for this reason that structural fire compartmentation, by the use of fire walls, fire doors, wired windows, and so on, is vital to prevent such uncontrolled spread of fire.

If the fire is contained its supplies of fuel and oxygen will be increasingly depleted by being burnt. Eventually the fire will be starved of fuel. This is the decay stage. The rate of burning falls away, and less heat is produced. Finally the fire will gradually die down and go out. Of course, most building fires will be extinguished in some other way long before this stage.

Few of us see a building fire develop and progress in this way. However, a large bonfire illustrates the natural burning process just discussed. It has adequate supplies of fuel and air. Initially the bonfire takes some minutes to develop into a good blaze. Then follows a period when the fire burns well, with lots of flames. The onlookers enjoy the spectacle. Sooner or later, depending upon the amount and type of fuel used to build the bonfire, the flames die down. The hot embers continue to burn, perhaps for many hours. The experienced bonfire builder aims to encourage his bonfire's development into a good blaze. He arranges the material so that there are open passageways into the heart of the pile of fuel, so as to admit a plentiful supply of air. He uses easily ignited materials in the base of the fire, so that as they burn the heat released will rise to the less inflammable materials above, and raise their temperature, so that they in turn become ignited. To ensure a long burn he uses plenty of solid wood to provide enough fuel.

A good bonfire demonstrates what not to do in a computer centre. Avoid having easily ignited materials, such as waste paper. Keep the fuel supply low, by using non-combustible furnishings. Keep doors closed and control the air supply.

The way materials aid the spread of fire is probably more important than their ease of ignition. It is usually only when a fire spreads to other sources of fuel that it becomes dangerous. (This would not apply where highly flammable materials are stored nearby.) The initial fire must generate more heat than is lost to the surroundings if it is to raise their temperature sufficiently for them to burn. For example, if a flame is applied to the edge of a thin sheet of material it will raise the local temperature, and perhaps ignite the local material. Some of the heat generated by the newly burning material will be conducted away by the surrounding material, some will be lost by radiation, and other heat will be lost by convection. If more heat is being generated by combustion than is lost in these ways the temperature of the neighbouring local material will rise sufficiently to ignite it. This neighbouring material in burning will generate yet more heat, and the substance will continue to burn, more and more of it being consumed. The heating is vital. When we want to ignite something we shelter it from cooling draughts. We learn by experience that it is easier to light a sheet of paper with a match by holding the paper vertically rather than horizontally. The flame applied at the bottom edge enables vertical convection of heat to aid the ignition process.

The fire must produce more heat than is required to ignite the adjacent material if it is to grow. If enough excess heat is generated to ignite more fuel, the fire will grow, and the process will accelerate. The local conditions determine whether or not a fire develops from an initial source of ignition like a burning cigarette end.

Once the fire is established in a room it will grow, provided fuel and oxygen are available. In a closed room the heat lost by the fire will heat up nearby materials. As the walls heat up they will re-radiate some of the heat back into the room and its contents. As the contents heat up they will become ignited, and the fire will spread.
Hot gases from the fire will rise to form a very hot layer near the ceiling. This layer is mainly the exhaust gas from the fire, which is short of oxygen. The fierce combustion uses up most of the available

oxygen. (This is why there is often better, more breathable air near the floor in a fire situation.)

There is a growing shortage of oxygen within the base of the fire. The hot gases rising from the fire therefore contain a growing proportion of unburnt gases distilled from the fuel. As they rise from the fire, and meet sufficient oxygen in the air above, these hot gases burn, producing flames. In normal growth the flames from the fire will soon reach the ceiling, and spread horizontally. Ceiling flames often extend surprisingly far across the underside of the hot layer of spent gases near the ceiling. In this hot layer the oxygen is already depleted. The unburnt gases therefore have to spread far to gain enough oxygen to burn, and produce flames. Such spread of flames often aids the development of the fire, especially where the ceiling or its lining is combustible.

The temperature of the hot gases rises to about 600 degrees C. At this stage the radiated heat is sufficient to ignite the remaining fuel. The fire suddenly grows much more fierce, a point which is termed "flashover".

The rate of combustion will usually be limited by the supply of air. Combustible gases are distilled from the fuel by the heat, but remain unburnt because of the lack of adequate supplies of oxygen in a closed space. Large amounts of hot unburnt gases will therefore be present in the room. These hot unburnt gases will spill out of the room through any available openings. The long flames reaching out of windows are produced by ignition of these hot unburnt gases when they reach the ample supply of oxygen in the free air.

If the doors and windows are closed, the growth of a room fire is often limited by lack of air. It may smoulder for hours. The nature of the fire may change dramatically if a door is opened, or if a window fails. Particular care is needed if the fire is in a small unoccupied room, like a store or cleaners' cupboards.

ONE MUST ALWAYS EXERCISE THE GREATEST CARE BEFORE OPENING A DOOR IF ONE SUSPECTS THAT THERE IS A FIRE ON THE OTHER SIDE. ALWAYS TEST THE DOOR FOR HEAT AND FUMES, AND PREFERABLY WAIT FOR EXPERT HELP.

TOXIC AND CORROSIVE GASES

These hot unburnt gases may spread quickly through ducts and hidden passages to remote parts of a building. Sound fire segregation is needed. Solid imperforate walls and floors with adequate fire resistance are essential to prevent this. Proper fire stopping of all openings and passages is vital. Hidden spread of hot gases through ducts and false ceilings presents a grave danger to people, since the lethal gases may arrive without warning in areas that appear to be remote and quite safe from the fire. Fire could be spread rapidly by an air conditioning system. Special protection against fire is always included in the design of such systems.

The fumes are also very bad for computers, office systems and their supporting media. Both heat and corrosive products of combustion can cause serious damage to computer equipment and media. Temperatures exceeding about 50 degrees C are likely to cause malfunctioning of electronic equipment. Magnetic media may be deformed and lose recorded data. Extensive damage will be caused by temperatures exceeding 150 degrees C. Floppy disks will be damaged by temperatures above 52 degrees C.

Combustion of plastic materials such as cable insulation and the backing of magnetic media produces corrosive products that damage internal components, switch contacts and connectors. PVC (polyvinyl chloride) is the most common plastic throughout the world. In buildings it is used for cable insulation, plumbing, floor and wall coverings, and all kinds of furniture and fittings. Unfortunately PVC produces hydrogen chloride gas when it burns, and this forms hydrochloric acid when it dissolves in water vapour. Burning PVC also produces the deadly carbon monoxide, and various other toxic substances depending upon what additives were included in the mix.

Carbon monoxide has always been a great killer. It is a colourless, odourless gas produced by the incomplete combustion of materials containing carbon, such as natural textiles, paper, wood, coal and oil. There is no warning of its presence in the air. (*Carbon monoxide* should not be confused with *carbon dioxide*. Carbon dioxide, though itself a suffocating gas, is not so serious a threat to life.) Carbon monoxide entering the blood through the lungs combines with the haemoglobin molecules in the oxygen-carrying red corpuscles of the blood to form carboxy-haemoglobin. Haemoglobin has a far higher affinity for carbon monoxide than for oxygen, and at equilibrium the carboxy-haemoglobin:oxy-haemoglobin ratio is 200 to 300 times higher than the carbon monoxide:oxygen ratio in the inspired air. The normal transport of oxygen is impeded, and the brain is starved of oxygen. Unconsciousness and irreversible brain damage follow. The more sensitive brain cells may survive no more than eight minutes deprivation of oxygen.

A concentration of 1.25 per cent of carbon monoxide is sufficient to cause unconsciousness after a couple of inhalations and death in three minutes. Much lower concentrations can be fatal, which is why the gas is so sinister. When it is combined with the usual mixture of toxic fumes from a modern fire the effect of carbon monoxide is multiplied. The brain is dulled, and reactions are unpredictable. Reduction of available oxygen diminishes muscular skill and control, and impairs judgement. Tiny concentrations are insidious in their effect.

Persons affected may be gradually brought to the very verge of unconsciousness without appreciating in the least degree that anything is wrong (Connor, 1984). They lose consciousness, quite without realising what is happening. They may then be overcome by the fumes from the fire, but they may well be dead long before the flames reach them.

Smouldering fires of wood or textiles are likely to produce large amounts of carbon monoxide. Tests in Germany showed that about one kilogram of smouldering textile – a largish cushion for instance – could produce 0.4 per cent carbon monoxide in a large living room. Such a concentration would allow less than ten minutes evacuation time.

In a fire situation, carbon dioxide will be present as well as carbon monoxide. Carbon dioxide affects breathing by increasing the depth of inspiration of the lungs. The effect is that a greater volume of air, and hence of the monoxide, is inhaled in a given time. This increases the toxic effect of a given concentration.

The plastic and latex foams used in upholstery produce masses of dense black toxic smoke as they burn. Exit routes are hidden and people become disoriented. Moreover, the fumes produce severe chest irritation and lung damage. Most current research work is aimed at minimising the possibility of the foam becoming ignited rather than preventing it from burning. There is little protection once it is burning.

The toxic fumes from such a fire, involving modern materials, can be lethal long before any flames are visible. People exposed to toxic fumes behave irrationally. Inhalation of carbon monoxide quickly impairs judgement.

In hazardous and unusual circumstances, people generally fail to appreciate the seriousness of their situation. The literature on fire protection is full of accounts of apparently stupid, even foolhardy behaviour by people involved in serious fires. In restaurant and nightclub fires diners have insisted on completing their meal, even when they could see the flames approaching. People fail to use the fire alarm points provided. Even when the alarm does sound, people wonder if it is a false alarm, and do not want to be the first to leave. Stubborn refusal to leave the premises is widespread. People fail to leave while escape routes are still safe, and then become trapped by the rapid development of a major fire.

Fire alarm procedures should take into account this effect on behaviour. Fire instructions should emphasise the urgency of prompt evacuation when fire is discovered. The aim should be to ensure that all occupants reach safety in no more than two and a half minutes. It can be argued that untrained and inexperienced people should not attempt to fight a fire, but should instead at once raise the alarm, call the fire brigade and ensure that evacuation of the building is speedy and complete. The professional fire brigade, knowing that all personnel are accounted for, can concentrate on attacking the fire. If people are missing, perhaps trapped by smoke, the firemen may risk their own lives to attempt a rescue.

3 The Building

LOCATION AND NEIGHBOURHOOD THREATS

The location of a computer installation has a significant impact upon its security. It is important to consider the neighbourhood, and the threats of fire that might arise from the activities of your own organisation or those of other nearby occupiers. Many industrial processes pose a significant hazard, and warehousing and transport depots have been the site of several major incidents in recent years. Many modern materials, especially solvents, paints and chemicals, and certain plastics, burn readily if ignited. A warehouse or depot containing a concentration of these materials may present a very large source of fuel. The amount and kind of combustible material available in a building is called the fire load. The fire load has a significant impact on the nature of any fire that does break out. The effects of fire load may well be overlooked, and a big fire load may exist without neighbours being aware of the fact, or the threat it poses to their own affairs. One computer installation was destroyed by a fire that started in an adjoining warehouse where many thousands of new telephone instruments were stored ready for delivery. Ample fuel to feed an unusually intense fire came from the plastic cases of the telephones, and from some large glass-fibre fabrications. The installation was wiped out in less than 30 minutes.

Supplies of heating oil, and of diesel fuel for standby generators or road vehicles are common hazards. One should not overlook gas mains in the vicinity of the site, especially old underground ones made of cast iron, rather than modern plastic. In frosty weather gas can seep beneath the ground into the subfloor or basement, giving rise to risk of fire or explosion. Heavy vehicles may crack gas mains unless the roadways are strong enough to give adequate protection.

A computer installation in an isolated rural situation may be less subject to neighbourhood risks than one in a congested urban industrial area. Against this one must consider the distance from the nearest fire station, and the number of fire appliances in the district that might be available to fight a serious blaze. In most urban areas the fire brigade will arrive within a few minutes of receiving an alarm call, and if needs be may be able to call upon dozens of appliances. In remote rural areas the appliances may have to travel many miles to reach the site. A large green field site near a prosperous small town may have fairly low risks.

BUILDING AND CONSTRUCTION

The relevant British Standard is *BS 5588: Part 3: 1983 Fire Precautions in the Design and Construction of Buildings.*

A clear explanation of fundamental principles of materials, structure and building design is given in *Book 8, Building Construction and Structural Fire Protection,* of the Home Office Manual of Firemanship. Another good source is *Aspects of Fire Precautions in Buildings* by Read and Morris (HMSO).

Both the *Fire Offices' Committee Recommendations (FOC)*and the British Standard code of practice *BS 6266: 1982 Fire Protection for Electronic Data Processing Installations* recommend that ideally the computer operation should be housed in a separate building of non-combustible construction reserved solely for the purpose. One would add that the building should be enclosed within a secure perimeter fence, to deter vandals and reduce the threat from arsonists. A dry moat will reduce the risks from attacks by suicide car bombers.

If, as is often the case, the computer area forms part of a larger building, it sould be separated from the rest of the building by walls of non-combustible construction, having appropriate fire resistance. The aim is to protect the computer installation from the effects of a fire that might occur elsewhere in the building. FOC recommends at least four hours fire resistance. If the rest of the premises in which the computer installation is housed are offices or similar accommodation, then the FOC requires walls of non-combustible construction with at least two hours fire resistance. The main floors should also be constructed of non-combustible materials and have a fire resistance of at least two hours.

BS 6266 differs in that it requires non-combustible walls and floors with one hour fire resistance for situations where the rest of the building is used for low fire load purposes, such as offices. For premises with a medium fire load, such as factories, it demands two hours, and for high fire load situations, such as furniture warehouses, it calls for four hours fire resistance.

The walls and floors should be imperforate, but where openings are essential they must be protected to retain the appropriate standard of fire resistance. All openings must be protected by fire break doors conforming to the FOC *Rules for the Construction and Installation of Fire Break Doors, Lobbies and Shutters.*

In walls with a fire resistance of one hour, BS 6266 requires self-closing doors with a fire resistance of one hour. In walls with two hour fire resistance it allows either a self-closing door with a fire resistance of one hour plus a steel roller shutter with a fire resistance of one hour held open by a fusible link on the side of the wall remote from the computer installation, or two self-closing doors with one hours fire resistance on either side of a lobby with a fire resistance of two hours. In the third case with a high fire load, where the construction has four hours fire resistance, the BS requirement is a self-closing door with a fire resistance of one hour protected on the two sides by a pair of roller shutters, each with a fire resistance of two hours, and each held open by fusible links on both sides of the opening.

If the computer area has external walls that might be exposed to an external fire then any windows should have wired glass in metal frames. Windows are best avoided in such situations.

Water damage is a serious risk if a fire should occur in the building, especially on a higher floor. Walls, floors and ceilings should be waterproof, and the main floor of the computer area should be raised above the surroundings, or be defended by sills (possibly with ramps) at all door openings.

All computer centres should have resources to hand to cope with minor flooding or spillages. Once an equipment unit has been powered-down, a large plastic (polythene) sheet can be spread over the cabinet to protect it from overhead water leaks. Special dust-free absorbent materials are available for use in clean areas, like computer rooms and media libraries. These leave no dust or other contamination, but will quickly absorb spills of water, oil and other liquids.

Ventilation and service ducts serving other areas should not pass through any part of the computer area, including the floor and ceiling voids. If such ducts are unavoidable they should be constructed as fire resisting shafts, so that any fire or smoke is contained within the shaft. Similarly any sections of ducting serving the computer area and external to it should likewise be treated as fire resisting shafts, to exclude fire from the duct. This should be done whether or not it is required by the building regulations.

Output and data handling areas often contain much paper. Rooms provided for engineering services or maintenance may have higher fire risks than ordinary offices. There may be soldering irons and special solvents or cleaners. Batteries for telephones or emergency lighting pose another threat. Waste disposal is often overlooked, but introduces vulnerabilities.

All such activities should be separated from the computer area by walls or partitions of non-combustible materials extending from the true structural floor to the soffit (underside) of the true structural floor or roof above. Such walls or partitions should have at least one hour fire resistance. Every opening should be protected by self-closing doors and/or shutters constructed from non-combustible materials.

All raised floors should be supported on non-combustible materials of adequate strength. Raised floors must retain integrity and provide adequate thermal insulation in the event of a fire developing in the void beneath the floor. The floor should be made from non-combustible material, or the underside should be surfaced with such material.

The linings for walls and ceilings should be of non-combustible materials. The materials used should not give rise to production of dust, or of toxic or corrosive fumes when heated.

Service pipes carrying water should not be brought into the computer area unless water is essential to operate the equipment. In such cases there should be an emergency cut-off for such supply pipes. Protection against water damage will be required, as discussed below.

Sometimes the computer area must be divided into rooms for operating convenience. Some extra fire protection can be achieved for media storage if the partitions have adequate fire resistance. The walls and floors forming such partitions should extend from true floor to true ceiling. It may be necessary to leave vent holes in the partitions above the ceiling or below the floor level to permit return air flow. All such hidden apertures should be protected by automatic self-closing doors or shutters with appropriate fire resistance.

Computers should not be installed in basements, because these have special fire risks. An installation would need special protection against flooding, and special access for fire-fighting personnel. There would have to be a special provision for removing smoke, and to prevent the accumulation of heat.

Computers should not be installed at high levels in multi-storey buildings because of the difficulties of access for fire fighting personnel and equipment. The ladders used by fire brigades have limited reach, typically only 90-100 feet. Traffic congestion in cities often requires that the means of escape must be designed discounting the possibility of rescue by the brigade using ladders.

Buildings are often equipped with dry-risers. The brigade can connect fire engines to the dry-risers and pump supplies of water to the higher floors. The hoses used to connect the dry-risers may be damaged by falling glass and debris.

Many computer rooms are designed without windows to prevent intrusion by vandals and other forms of attack. Consideration should be given to providing effective means of allowing escape of heat, and escape routes for personnel. All computer areas should be equipped with adequate means to extract smoke directly into the open air.

Accurate and up-to-date floor plans should be available outside the computer area at a suitable control point, where they will be available for reference by fire officers who may be called to a fire incident.

ESCAPE ROUTES

In a fire emergency the aim must be to permit everyone to reach safety in less than two and a half minutes. The importance of this time is based on tests on fires involving plastics, especially polyurethane and PVC, which reach maximum severity in a few minutes. After this time, due to the heat and toxicity of the dense black smoke produced, it is virtually impossible for anyone to escape from affected areas without injury.

People tend to go out of any building by the route they used to enter it, and this should be taken into account in planning escape routes.

The Home Office *Guide to the Fire Precautions Act 1971. Number 3. Offices, Shops and Railway Premises discusses escape* routes, and states that it is not possible to set hard and fast rules. The Greater London Council's *Code of Practice: Means of Escape in Case of Fire* provides comprehensive details of all aspects, and is well worth consulting.

Ideally there should be at least two escape routes from every part of the premises, preferably leading in oppposite directions.

The *Guide* considers means of escape in three stages:

1. Travel within rooms
2. Travel from rooms to a stairway or final exit
3. Travel within stairways and to final exits.

It makes recommendations about distance of travel, which should be measured as the actual distance to be travelled between any point in a building and the nearest final exit, or door to a protected escape route, or door for means of escape in a compartment wall.

The *Guide* recommends that in offices the distance of travel should not exceed 45 metres from any point where escape is possible in more than one direction. The distance should be no more than 18 metres where escape is in one direction only. These distances are not very far, when you take obstructing furniture and equipment into account.

Exit routes should be clearly signposted with approved safety signs. All exit routes should be fitted with automatic emergency lighting, which should be regularly tested to ensure its continued efficiency. Dead ends, such as store cupboards, should be kept locked, and be clearly labelled.

Escape routes are often protected by a number of self-closing fire check doors at intervals along corridors, and at staircase landings. The doors are arranged in such a way as to prevent any spread of smoke and fumes along corridors and up stairways. Without this protection alternative escape routes may become impassable. Moreover the fire itself may spread very rapidly to all parts of a building if the doors are not shut.

Ordinary fire check doors are often wedged open, so that they are quite useless. This can be avoided by installing self-closing doors, normally latched open by an electromagnet linked to the fire detection system. When a fire is detected the latches are released and all the doors close. There is no temptation ever to wedge them, because in normal use people find the doors are open. In such a system the doors are normally released during closed hours. A useful precaution is to have an intumescent fire seal in a groove round the edges of all doors.

Emergency exit doors to the outside should be fitted with means for release in an emergency. Panic bars, if properly maintained, are probably safer than either glass bolts or keys in glass-fronted boxes. Doors can be protected by an alarm circuit to ensure that they are not used without authorisation, and that they are not left open by accident. This may be important if the door opens on to a public street.

Where doors are controlled by an automatic access control system it is vital to ensure that the system is fail-safe. Normally the door strikes are latched electrically. The system will be arranged so that the strike is released when power is removed. In the event of an alarm, power is dropped at all the doors, so that free passage is available. Controlled doors should always have a mechanical override, so that the door can be opened with a key or lever protected by a break-glass panel.

FIRE-STOPPING BULKHEADS

Fire-resistant bulkheads are needed where cables pass through walls and partitions. Holes for passage of cables and pipes must be fire stopped to maintain the integrity and overall fire resistance of walls, floors and partitions. Particular vigilance is needed to ensure that fire stopping is reinstated after any alteration to cables in existing installations. Do not overlook telephone and data communications circuits. Small holes and even tiny cracks can admit seriously damaging leakage of smoke and fumes in the event of fire. Fires in computer areas often involve PVC or polyurethane cable insulation, and significant amounts of smoke can be spread before the seal becomes effective. Ensure that cables are arranged tidily and that they are not bunched tightly together, since this may seriously degrade their current-carrying capacity.

Fire stopping at walls and floors can be provided in several ways. One common method uses a number of slabs of specially prepared high-density mineral wool, which are formed to fit closely against the reveals of the opening in the structure, and round the pipes, cables and cable supports. The whole bulkhead is then coated on both sides with intumescent paint, which greatly expands when heated. Sometimes the paint is extended a short distance along the cables. The intumescent paint systems need a rise in temperature to cause the expansion that is needed to ensure a smoke tight seal. Smoke alone does not cause expansion of intumescent materials.

In another system the fire-stopping bulkheads are formed from mortar formulated from specially fire-resistant materials. Such stopping tends to crack in time, especially if there is movement of the cable supports. Good workmanship is needed to make such stopping effective, especially in confined and awkward spaces.

Where water and gas resistance is needed a modular cable gland system can be used. This consists of a steel frame into which a series of fire-resisting blocks can be fitted. The blocks are shaped to accept a wide range of cable and pipe diameters. Solid (blank) blocks can be fitted in other parts of the frame to provide spare capacity to allow for later expansion. The complete assembly is compressed to make it watertight and gastight.

In another system the fire stopping consists of two fire-retardant boards placed at the two faces of the wall, and these act as dams to retain a special silicone foam used to fill the space between. The silicone foam is mixed in situ, and expands approximately threefold in volume, so that it is forced into every sealable space within the cavity before it can solidify. Even tightly bunched cables can be sealed-off, though they should be avoided. It is relatively easy to remove redundant cables, or to add new ones and to reinstate the seal with more foam. Seals can be installed in fairly inaccessible spaces.

A versatile system of fire stopping is formed from small bags each filled with special materials. The bags can be stuffed tightly round the cables and their supports, rather like small sandbags. It is easy to adjust the fire stopping when cables are added or removed, as is so often the case. The method could be particularly useful during installation and construction when fire threats are often higher than normal. Another advantage is that the cables are unaffected by applied sealants, as happens with some other systems.

WATER DAMAGE

Water may be used to extinguish fire in a computer centre or other parts of a building. This is a serious hazard. The ceiling of the computer area must be waterproof. Floor voids must have floors sloping towards water channels and drains, equipped with pumps if necessary. This is especially important with today's powerful water-cooled central processors. The walls of the computer area should have sills, or its floor should be raised above the surrounding level, to prevent ingress of water. Where holes are made in the walls for entry of cables these must be made good to prevent entry of fire or water, as discussed above. A check for potential problems should be part of periodic site inspections.

The computer system might be located towards the centre of the floor in a multi-storey building, rather than at the outside, so as to afford it some protection from water overflowing from fire fighting on higher floors.

Drains and channels should be employed throughout the building to ensure that, no matter where the computer room is located, fire fighting on a floor above or elsewhere on the site will not result in leakage into the computer area or its associated plant rooms or electrical substations. Protective waterproof plastic sheets should be available in the computer area so that the equipment cabinets can be protected if water should leak from above.

Supplies of dustless non-toxic absorbent material should be available to trap spillages of water or other liquid.

4 Electric Power Supplies

INSTALLATION

All electrical work should comply with the current edition of the *Regulations for the Electrical Equipment of Buildings* issued by the Institution of Electrical Engineers. Cables and equipment should be of the correct size and be rated conservatively for the loads likely to be encountered.

Standby generators, motor alternator sets and oil-filled equipment should be installed remote from the computer area and from the air-conditioning plant, and should be fire separated from them. The main distribution cables used should be of appropriate size for the distances involved, to avoid excessive voltage drop.

The main electrical distribution system should be so arranged that another source of supply can be connected to it in an emergency to feed the distribution system to the computer area and its associated air conditioning system. A mobile generator might then be brought into service if the main supply were disrupted by fire or other disaster. Some installations will have standby power supplies from generators driven by prime movers like diesels or gas turbines. Others will have uninterruptable power supplies, with floating batteries.

Where power distribution cables are run under a false floor, the cables should be protected against mechanical damage. Cables can be steel armoured, mineral insulated copper covered (micc or "pyro"). BS 6266: 1982 recommends that underfloor junction boxes should be avoided wherever possible. If essential, they should be of metal, or flame-retardant plastic, completely enclosed and be easily accessible. (Many cable fires start with local heating at a loose terminal.) The underfloor area should be protected against ingress of water. The electrical installation might be raised above the subfloor to protect it from minor floodwater. Where modular false floors are used, appropriate floor lifters should be available and readily accessible.

Socket outlets should have individual indicator lamps, and should be so mounted as to preclude the ingress of dust and debris. Sockets should be sited to minimise the need to use extension leads for test equipment or cleaning machines. Adequate numbers of sockets should be provided. BS 6266: 1982 strongly recommends that socket outlets should be excluded from voids.

It may be desirable to protect special "clean" computer power supplies from misuse, perhaps by using special socket outlets and plugs. This would minimise problems of overloading by abnormal loads such as floor-cleaning machines.

There should be master emergency cut-off switches for the power supplies both to the computer system and to the air conditioning system. Switches should be located near the main operators' console and near the exit door(s) to the computer area, and preferably outside, perhaps near the fire officer's display panel. These switches should be clearly labelled, and shrouded or protected by glass to guard against accidental or malicious operation. Instructions for using the switches should be posted alongside. The power is restored using the normal controls, which will usually be protected by a key-operated switch.

In large computer systems supporting major on-line networks, the design of power isolation circuits will demand special care. The need to maintain an operational system will often override the need to drop the power in a potential fire situation. Automatic time-delayed circuit breakers are much to be preferred, and have the additional benefit that they minimise the chance of human interference.

There should be a main isolator for use by the fire brigade, controlling all power supplies in the computer area, except lighting and smoke extraction. The switch should be labelled Fire Emergency Electrical Isolation Switch, and may be protected by a glass-fronted box.

A suitable emergency lighting system should be installed, and tested regularly to keep it in efficient working order.

CABLES

Immense numbers of pipes and cables are left unprotected in modern buildings, even in computer rooms. Fire can often spread unhindered along flammable cable insulation, which results in the release of toxic and corrosive gases. One should bear in mind that many computer room fires start in power cables, often in underfloor voids or ducts. BS 6266 recommends that all cables should be flame retardant to comply with the requirements of BS 4066 *Tests on Electrical Cables under Fire Conditions*. Cable ducts should have effective fire-stopping barriers where they pass through structural fire-stopping walls and floors (as discussed in Chapter 3).

Polyvinyl chloride (PVC) is used extensively for all kinds of cables. In its original form it is rigid and almost incombustible, but for use in cable insulation, and many other applications, a plasticiser must be added to give it flexibility. If it is involved in a fire it burns because of the presence of the plasticiser, and propagates flame. PVC cables can be rendered fire retardant by incorporating antimony oxide and phosphate or chloride plasticisers. They are relatively expensive. Although not themselves combustible, the cables have some nasty side effects if they are actually burnt in a fire, because they give off masses of dense corrosive fumes. This can impede evacuation and fire fighting.

Special cables are being marketed that are insulated with materials which do not contain halogens, sulphur or nitrogen. These new materials give off virtually no corrosive or toxic products in the event of a fire, apart from some carbon monoxide, which is almost unavoidable in any fire. New installations should consider using them.

Cables can be coated with intumescent paint. (Intumescent materials expand very greatly in volume when they are heated.) The intumescent paint expands if there is a significant rise in temperature, and thus protects the cable. Care must be taken to ensure that such an intumescent coating does not seriously degrade the current-carrying capacity of the cables. The cables should be derated to take account of the coating.

Another device is to enclose the cabling in trunking protected by layers of water-filled bags. The water boils if there is a fire, and the cable temperature rises little beyond 100 degrees C.

Mice and rats often chew plastic cable insulation. Any infestation should be tackled before danger from short circuits can arise.

5 Air Conditioning

SYSTEM DESIGN

The Fire Offices' Committee Recommendations advise use of a separate air conditioning system located outside the computer area.

The air-conditioning supply to computer areas must be entirely separate from any other system, otherwise there is grave risk of carrying heat, smoke and fumes into thc computer rooms from a fire occurring elsewhere in the building. For the same reason the ducting supplying other areas must not pass through the computer area unless it is adequately protected, for instance by a fire-resistant stack. The main duct on the delivery side of the fan should be protected by an automatic fire alarm system. All ducts and trunking should incorporate automatic fire shutters or dampers at the segregation walls and floors. These are normally held open either by a fusible link, or by an electromagnetic device linked to the fire detection and alarm system and also arranged to close if the electric supply fails. There should also be manual means for operating such shutters and dampers. Fusible links operate at a much later stage in a fire than do smoke detectors, and they therefore offer less immediate protection to people and equipment. Smoke detectors tend to be more susceptible to false alarms. There should be easy means for resetting all dampers after operation.

The air conditioning system should maintain a positive air pressure in the computer area, so as to prevent ingress of fumes from outside. The system should be designed to avoid the recirculation of smoke from a fire in a plant room or auxiliary area into the main computer area. The main air intakes should be so sited that they are unlikely to introduce smoke from a fire elsewhere in the neighbourhood.

The computer area should be fitted with adequate means for quickly removing smoke. Where gas flooding systems are fitted there should be provision for removing the extinguishant after the proper holding time. The design should ensure that ducts intended for smoke extraction cannot be closed-off accidentally by dampers or shutters.

Normally there should be automatic or controlled shut-off of air-conditioning fans in the event of a fire alarm. However, in large on-line systems there may be an overriding need to maintain the operation of the system, except in a serious fire situation. It is essential that the equipment is correctly powered-down before the cooling effect of the air conditioning system is removed. There may be a rapid rise of temperature even when power has been removed. Considerable heat may be stored within the components of modern electronic equipment, and without the cooling effect of the flow of air the temperature inside the equipment may rise appreciably. Correct sequencing and timing is essential to avoid unnecessary damage to the equipment. There must also be manually operated and suitably labelled switches which can be shut down the air-conditioning system. These should be located near the operators' console and the main exit door. Additional controls are usually provided near the fire alarm panel in larger installations. Manual controls for the air conditioning and smoke evacuation systems should be available outside the computer area, secured against unauthorised tampering.

Where gas-flooding systems are used the air-conditioning system must be stopped before the extinguishant is discharged, otherwise it will be dispersed and rendered ineffective. The doors should also be closed to ensure that extinguishant is not lost, and secured to prevent re-entry of personnel from outside unitl the area has been declared safe by the senior fire officer. Emergency exit doors from such an area require special consideration. They should preferably be self-closing. It may be possible to interlock the exit doors with the release system for the gas-flooding system, so that the gas cannot be discharged until the doors are closed. Proper advice should be sought.

Combustible materials should not be used in ductings, linings, vapour barriers, coatings, acoustic treatments or insulation. The materials used should not produce dust, or corrosive or toxic fumes when heated. Air filters should be non-combustible, and they should be cleaned or replaced at regular intervals to eliminate fluff and other combustible materials.

PLANT ROOMS

Plant rooms should be separated from the computer area by a construction with a minimum fire resistance of one hour. The plant room should not contain fire hazards, such as oil-filled electrical equipment or combustible waste. Good housekeeping is essential, and plant rooms should be locked to prevent unauthorised interference. All plant should be properly maintained to avoid danger of overheating from wear, lack of lubrication, or faulty adjustment.

Coolant systems used with air conditioning should be fitted with an alarm to give warning if the coolant falls below the recommended level.

UNIT AIR CONDITIONERS

When unit air conditioners are used they should be protected by an automatic fire alarm system. Units should have non-combustible construction. Any acoustic or thermal insulation used in the units should have good combustion-resistant properties. It should not generate toxic or corrosive fumes, or dust. Units should be fitted with thermal cut-outs and alarms to monitor overheating of bearings or motors, and failure of fans or blockage of filters.

WATER SUPPLIES

Any water supplies and header tanks associated with humidifiers in air-conditioning systems should be located so that they are protected against freezing in winter. They should be sited so that leakage or overflow could not cause flooding in the computer area or its associated plant and equipment rooms, and thus affect electrical equipment. Cooling towers and ponds should be protected against growth of algae or weeds that might block or impede circulation. In districts with hard water, care should be taken to avoid built-up of limescale. One installation in Kent was destroyed in 1977 when such deposits prevented a pressure relief safety valve from functioning correctly. A large hot-water calorifier exploded beneath the computer room.

SUPPLEMENTARY HEATING

Supplementary heating systems are sometimes installed in computer rooms to protect the equipment against low temperatures caused by failure of the air-conditioning system in cold weather. Care should be taken to ensure that only flameless, black heat is used. Supplementary heaters should be permanently fixed and be so sited that they cannot be obstructed to introduce an unanticipated fire risk.

6 Building Contents

INTRODUCTION

Furnishings and fittings should be selected taking account of their fire-resistance properties. They should preferably be non-combustible. For example, steel shelving should be preferred to that made from timber or particle boards.Decorative treatments selected for walls and ceilings should not be such as to encourage the spread of flame.

COMPUTER ROOMS

Computer equipment itself contains much plastic, including resin-impregnated circuit boards. The cases of VDU terminals may be moulded from flammable plastic. Cases and reels for magnetic tape, and the backing of the tape itself, may be flammable plastic. There will be supplies of continuous stationery, and printer ribbons. Electrical equipment, switchgear, and junction boxes will probably contain combustible material. The engineers will have supplies of cleaning fluids, lubricating fluids and aerosols. Office cleaners may have supplies of floor or furniture wax. There will also be waste, particularly from computer output and despatch operations like guillotining. Scrap is often easily ignited, and may present a serious hazard without good housekeeping.

OFFICE FURNITURE

Office furniture today is often made from non-traditional materials, including many plastics, adhesives, expanded rubber and plastic foams, laminated particle boards, and other sheet materials. Special synthetic finishes are used. These materials bring new fire hazards into office buildings. Computer centres are affected by this change just as much as other offices. Normal office furniture is provided for managers and supervisors, as well as for clerical functions like data control. There may be a reception area furnished with comfortable seating for visitors. Operations staff, especially in larger centres, will have separate rest areas, and perhaps a kitchen.

Furniture can be divided into two groups: soft furnishings, including carpets, curtains, and upholstery; and non-flexible furniture, such as tables, shelves and cupboards. Soft furnishings are often easily ignited, whereas other furnishings may burn only when the fire has gained a hold. Today upholstered furniture is usually made of textile materials and foam, rather than traditional stuffing and springing. The heat and gases from the burning soft furnishings would be lethal for nearby personnel.

Furnishings and fittings are usually selected on their aesthetic qualities. Their fire attributes are rarely considered. The fire attributes of a building with excellent structural fire protection may be seriously degraded by an unwise choice of materials for the furnishings and decorations.

SOFT FURNISHINGS

The fire resistance of a textile is affected by its surroundings. The inherent fire-resistance properties of textiles can be divided into three broad types, though these are greatly affected by other factors, such as the structure of the fabric, or various finishes that may be applied. A few fibres, such as wool, resist burning. Some fibres, such as polyamide (eg Nylon) and polyester (eg Trevira, Terylene), burn well but melt away from a fire. The burning droplets produced may ignite materials below. Other fibres such as cellulosics (cotton, linen, viscose) are easily ignited and burn readily. Polyacrylonitrile "acrylic" (eg Acrilan, Orlan, Courtelle, Dralon) and polypropylene also burn readily.

The weight and structure of the fabric affects its flammability. Lightweight and open structures tend to burn more readily, because oxygen is more easily available. The behaviour of a textile fabric is difficult to predict, especially when different fibres are blended together.

Chemical treatments can be applied to fabrics to increase their fire-resistance properties. Treated fabrics tend to cost more. The effectiveness of these treatments depends to some extent upon the expertise with which they are applied. Some treatments, based on borax, boric acid or ammonium salts, are rendered ineffective by laundering, though they may be unaffected by correct dry cleaning. Other treatments, using phosphorus-based chemicals (eg Proban and Pyrovatex), are more durable.

Wool is normally regarded as a fire-resistant fabric. The International Wool Secretariat has a finish called Zirpro which will increase its fire resistance. The treatment adds at least ten per cent to the cost of typical furnishing fabrics.

Leather is inherently fire resistant. The flammability of PVC varies with the amounts of fire-resistant chemicals introduced into the composition of the original extrusion mix.

Flexible polyurethane foam and rubber latex foam are used in upholstery. Both burn readily if ignited, and produce a wide range of toxic gases. The threat posed by these foams is generally acknowledged, but no inexpensive alternative is available. The approach at present is to prevent ignition, and to try to slow down the rate of fire propagation, rather than to control the toxic gases that are produced once the material is on fire.

In upholstered furniture it is the properties of the combination of the covering material with the underlying foam that matters, rather than the behaviour of the two components separately. Sometimes a barrier material can be introduced between the outer fabric and the foam. Much attention has been given to smouldering cigarettes and lighted matches as ignition sources for upholstered furniture. In theory these sources are relevant for well-conducted computer rooms, though the hazard may exist in reception and rest areas, as well as in ordinary offices.

Curtains and their linings should be made from fire-resistant materials. Curtains offer a ready path for fire to reach the ceiling, and should be avoided in vulnerable locations.

Carpets, being horizontal, offer much less rapid spread of flames than do curtains. The main hazard from carpets and carpet tiles is often the backing material, or the underlay. Foam rubber, often used for underlays, will burn readily and generate masses of toxic smoke. Some carpet tiles have a bitumen backing which burns to produce thick black smoke.

Stacking chairs are made from many different materials, such as moulded wood or plastics. The appearance gives little clue to the material used to form the seat. This may introduce unexpected risks, if such chairs are used in rest areas. Tests have shown that single chairs are often difficult to ignite. Stacks of chairs often burn better. This is because the burning material from the topmost chair melts, and, instead of dropping harmlessly to the floor, it falls on the chairs below, thus igniting the whole stack.

WASTE AND OTHER MATTERS

Waste bins should be made of metal, preferably with automatic lids. They should be emptied regularly to a secure container outside the building.

Smoking should be discouraged except in protected areas. If smoking is permitted the performance of fire detectors is degraded. In areas where smoking is permitted plenty of large deep ashtrays should be provided. The contents of ashtrays should be safely discarded, and not be mixed with other waste.

Only media essential for immediate use should be kept within the computer room. Such media should be kept in enclosed metal racks. Immediate supplies of stationery should be kept neatly boxed with no loose sheets.

Cleaning materials and engineers' supplies should be kept in closed metal cupboards.

Soldering irons pose special risks. A proper stand must always be used. These are designed to dissipate heat safely from each particular type of iron. Soldering irons should never be left unattended when hot.

Outdoor clothes should be kept in individual steel lockers.

In kitchens and rest areas, a naked flame should be avoided

wherever possible. Automatic electric kettles should be provided. Automatic microwave cookers probably entail less risk than normal gas or electric cookers, grills and hobs.

7 Protection of Records

HEAT AND SMOKE

Magnetic media and paper are easily damaged by smoke and heat. Temperatures exceeding 60 degrees C are likely to damage magnetic media, whereas good paper will survive about 130 degrees C. Floppy disks are more susceptible to damage than other magnetics, and 52 degrees C is the usual limit quoted. Incidentally, exposure to strong sunshine can produce significantly higher temperatures in summertime. A concentration of small computers, or office systems equipment, in an office may generate enough heat to produce unacceptable temperatures, especially in hot weather. The high ambient temperatures achieved may not be tolerated by the equipment, and may produce erratic behaviour.

BACK-UP COPIES

The FOC recommends that the amount of records kept within the computer area should be minimised. This is commendable practice for traditional batch-processing systems. It helps to reduce the fire load in the computer area. Other data that is not currently needed would be kept elsewhere in a safer place.

Many large modern systems have massive on-line "disk farms", containing almost all the installation's data and programs. These are in continuous use, and so cannot be taken away as FOC recommends. It follows that such disk farms should have very good fire precautions. If possible the disks should be distributed over a number of rooms with proper fire separation.

Every computer centre tries to protect essential files by creating back-up copies of master data files, program libraries and other important information. In batch systems the "grandfather, father, son" system is traditionally used. Modern data and file management systems use other methods. There may be incremental dumps of the changes in the filed data. Transaction files may be kept, perhaps with "before" and "after" images of the data. The data can then be reconstructed from some checkpoint dump, using the after images. Whatever method is used to secure the operational data it is vital that copies are kept safe against destruction by fire, or other hazards.

Several copies of the back-up data are usually made for essential files. The back-up copies should be transferred as soon as practicable to safe storage.

There should be secure storage facilities both on-site and at a remote location. The two kinds of storage are complementary, not alternatives.

DATA SAFES

Properly fire-certified data safes, or fire- and moisture-resistant vaults, should be available on-site. If vaults are used they should be equipped with suitable fire extinguishers, fire alarm points and distress alarms for personnel.

Any safe used for media must be a data safe. Safes intended for paper and other valuables afford inadequate protection against the danger of high temperatures. Data safes have much more thermal insulation than standard safes. The extra insulation and perhaps protection against smoke is often provided by fitting a special cabinet inside the safe. Look for doors that have good seals to prevent the ingress of smoke, fumes and moisture. Fire fighting often results in water damage.

A data safe should be so sited that it is unlikely to be buried if the building collapses after a fire. For preference it should be sited near an outside wall and doorway, so that it may be salvaged more easily following a major incident. Several days may elapse before a safe can be recovered after a fire. Always call the safemaker or an expert locksmith to open a safe after an incident. Never permit ordinary salvage personnel to attempt this without such expert advice. Unthinking salvage personnel have opened safes with flame cutting gear. Magnetic tapes have been destroyed in this way after surviving serious fires inside a safe.

Safes should be kept closed and locked except when media is actually being inserted or removed. If the doors are left open the contents might be contaminated by a sudden inrush or seepage of smoke before the doors could be closed. Safes have suffered severe blows in fire incidents, either from falling masonry and debris, or by the safe falling through to another floor. In one case the safe handle was dislodged, thus releasing the unlocked door, and exposing the contents.

OFF-SITE STORAGE

On-site facilities should be used to protect copies of newly-created files, and to provide immediate back-up for the working copies.

The on-site facilities should be backed-up by secure off-site storage, preferably a mile or two away. The copies held at a remote site will be available for use immediately after a fire. It may be several days before salvage crews reach and recover the on-site data safe. There should be three copies of each vital file, one for immediate use, a second safely held in on-site secure storage, and a third at the secure remote location.

There should be proper schedules and procedures for moving files between the three locations. Secure transport should be used. Consideration should be given to safe handling of media and documentation at each end of the journey, and to its protection from inclement weather. Records should be held at each location showing precisely where the several copies of each vital file are held. From time to time these records at each location should be checked against the actual holding so as to ensure that the procedures are working properly.

Some systems generate the movement instructions for media directly from librarian data held within the operating system. Instructions produced in this way are more likely to reflect the actual situation than instructions generated from manual records.

There may be daily or twice daily runs to move media to and from the remote site. The schedules should be arranged in such a manner that at least one copy of each vital file is in secure storage at all times.

The latest versions should be in secure storage before earlier ones are brought back. Data that is generated after the last journey to the remote store will be somewhat vulnerable until copies can be transported on the next journey. Special care needs to be taken to minimise exposure in this way, otherwise the possible loss of data may be very great.

At some smaller installations back-up copies of disks are taken home, perhaps by the manager, to give some off-site protection. The back-ups must be properly safeguarded from tampering and damage, perhaps by children, if this is done. Domestic circumstances do not always afford satisfactory conditions for media storage.

OTHER VITAL SUPPLIES

No computer installation can survive for long without adequate documentation. All vital documentation should be secured against loss by fire. There should be adequate operations, program and system specifications for every application and systems software item.

One effective method is to use computer-based text preparation and documentation systems, so that all documentation is automatically secured like every other file on magnetic media. The documentation will then be backed-up automatically in the off-site storage, and it is much more likely to be up-to-date. One site without such off-site protection lost almost everything in a flood. They reported that it was not easy to reconstruct the lost data, but that recreating the systems and programming documentation was nearly impossible.

Supplies of special stationery (invoices, payslips, etc) must be held at an off-site store to allow for back-up running in case of disaster. There should be sufficient quantity to supply the installation's estimated needs until deliveries of new supplies can be obtained. The supplies at the remote site must be rotated with new stock, thus avoiding staleness.

Small stocks of standard media, ribbons and other consumables should be available off-site, for emergency use.

8 Fire Detection

AUTOMATIC FIRE DETECTION

An automatic fire-detection system may not be needed if the installation is always manned, or where the power supply is always disconnected when the premises are left unoccupied. It may be held that any outbreak of fire is likely to be detected quickly by the staff. However, many installations will contain enclosed and hidden spaces, voids and ducts, where a fire might start without being observed. Floor voids and store rooms will need detectors even where the installation is fully manned.

The FOC recommends that the entire installation should be protected by an automatic fire-alarm system approved by the Committee and installed generally in accordance with the Committee's rules for Automatic Fire Alarm Installations. The system should be capable of detecting the presence of a fire and possibly automatically actuating the quenching system. Normally, the fire-detection system should also automatically disconnect the power supply, in case the cause is electrical; shut down the air-conditioning system to avoid aggravation of the fire, and (where gas-flooding systems are installed) to allow the necessary gas concentration to be achieved; close the fire dampers and shutters; and operate self-closing doors to avoid the spread of fire and smoke.

The design of a fire-detection system should be entrusted to those competent in the field. The system should be maintained regularly by the installer, preferably under a maintenance contract.

The fire-alarm system should be capable of detecting a fire at an early stage, and also have well-placed manual call points. Good practice is to have "Fire Points" which are elaborated notice boards which contain not only notices of fire and safety regulations, but manual alarm control points and other manual emergency controls. Such fire points would also have fire extinguishers with instructions for use. Above eye level and visible from a distance would be the sign "FIRE POINT".

Immediately a fire is detected, appropriate audible alarms should be sounded of adequate volume to be heard above the normal background noise. Fire alarms should be distinct from any other kinds of warning or alarm. Many installations will have warnings for other alarm conditions. When a fire alarm sounds people must be in no doubt that it is a fire alarm. They should at once evacuate the premises and assemble at the designated fire assembly point.

In large establishments, two-stage fire alarms are often used. The first stage is an "alert" signal (usually intermittent) which need not be treated as a signal for general evacuation. Stage 2 is an "evacuation" signal (usually continuous); which means evacuate immediately and assemble at the appointed place. In large buildings the evacuation signal might be given in part of a building while other parts are receiving an alert.

The advantage of the two-stage system is that business interruptions due to false alarms are minimised. The alarm can be investigated after the stage 1 alert has been sounded. Evacuation or all-clear instructions can then be given as appropriate.

RAISING THE ALARM

If a fire is detected the alarm must be raised at once. The fire brigade must be called. There should be clear rules about how this is to be done. An automatic system may be connected to the fire brigade or to a central fire alarm station. It is possible to arrange such a link all the time or to have it operational only when the premises are unoccupied. Direct lines have been used for many years. It is possible to have the fire alarm connected to the calling service using a normal telephone exchange line with automatic dialling.

The importance of raising the alarm and calling the fire brigade cannot be emphasised too strongly. Minutes matter. Calling the fire brigade twice is far better than no call, or a call that is too late. The newly finished Maltings Concert Hall at Snape, near Aldeburgh in Suffolk, burned for 30 minutes watched by a crowd of sightseeing holiday makers. No one called the fire brigade. The hall was burned down. At the Summerlands disaster in the Isle of Man the brigade was not called for 35 minutes after the fire was first noticed.

An automatic fire-detection system may give rise to operational problems if it immediately shuts down power supplies and air-conditioning systems. The system should be arranged to minimise the possibility and inconvenience of false alarms. When the premises are manned, appropriate decisions can be taken by the senior person present at the time. Another possibility is to require that at least two independent detector circuits should indicate an alarm condition before any disruptive action is initiated. This will help to avoid inconvenience caused by malicious triggering of a detector, or by electrical malfunction. Fire detectors can be affected adversely by odd environmental conditions.

During those periods when the computer is manned, automatic shut down could entail heavy losses, especially in recovery of the operational system. It is desirable to arrange either for graceful manual shut down of operations in a predetermined manner, or to have automatic purpose-designed power-down circuitry. Removing power supplies by dropping circuit breakers at the power distribution unit is likely to harm the equipment.

DETECTOR TYPES AND THEIR LOCATION

An excellent description of the various kinds of fire detector is given in Part 2 of *Book 9, Fire Protection of Buildings* in the Home Office Manual of Firemanship.

The function of a fire detector is to detect one or more changes in the protected environment that would indicate the development of a fire condition. Detectors are usually mounted at ceiling level or in air ducts. Four stages in the development of a fire can be detected:

1. After ignition, when invisible products of combustion are being produced.

2. When visible smoke is produced.
3. When flames and heat are being produced.
4. When there is a significant rise in temperature produced by the fire.

In a computer centre, early detection of any fire is vital. The ionisation detector can signal the presence of invisible products of combustion, generally long before there is any visible smoke or flame.

Optical smoke detectors rely on the visible smoke particles produced by a fire. One type depends on the scattering of a light beam that is produced by these smoke particles. (This is the phenomenon that makes sunbeams visible beneath the shade of the trees in a forest.) Another kind of optical smoke detector relies on the obscuration of a beam of light produced by the smoke particles.

Flames from a blaze produce visible light and infra-red radiation. Radiation detectors are used in warehouses and other locations, but not usually in computer areas, because the response to a fire would be too late.

Heat detectors usually depend upon expansion of gases, liquids or solids, though fusion (melting) of metals, and electrical effects are also used.

Some heat detectors are arranged to operate when the ambient temperature reaches a pre-set value. Others are so arranged that they respond also to a rapid rise in temperature, such as might occur in a fire situation. These are called heat rise detectors, and are often used to protect ancilliary areas in computer centres. A common type has two bi-metallic strip thermostats. One of these is thermally insulated from the surroundings by a thick plastic sheath, while the other is protected only by a very thin metal cover. The second thermostat therefore responds more quickly than the insulated one to any change in ambient temperature. The detector is arranged so that this difference in response operates an electrical contact.

The normal starting point for fire officers and fire insurance surveyors is British Standard 5839: Part 1: 1980, *Fire Detection and Alarm Systems in Buildings.*

BS 6266: 1982, *Fire Protection for Electronic Data Processing Installations,* gives recommendations for types of fire detectors and their spacing and location. Heat detectors are not recommended for computer rooms because their response is too slow to detect fires at an early stage. Point-type smoke detectors are preferred for the computer area. Two different principles are employed in smoke detectors. The ionisation chamber detector is very sensitive to flaming fires, and has commonly been installed in computer rooms for many years. It will detect a fire in a waste paper basket before you can see smoke coming from the flamimg combustion. The optical scatter type of detector responds well to smouldering fires, which are not well-detected by the ionisation type of detector. Overheating PVC produces very large white particles of smoke, which are visible when the temperature is only about 100 degrees C. The ionisation chamber will not detect this fire until the smoke density is very high indeed, but it will respond well once the temperature rises to 350-400 degrees C. BS 6266 therefore recommends a mixture of equal numbers of the two kinds of smoke detector.

A high density of detectors is needed, because the computer equipment can be damaged by the smoke and fumes from a very small fire. The rapid circulation of air produced by the air-conditioning system tends to reduce the detection capability of the instruments, simply because the products of combustion are diluted. On the other hand, air conditioning has a scavenging effect if it is properly balanced, and will tend to sweep the entire air space quite quickly. In an EDP equipment room with 3 metre ceiling height, the recommended density is not less than one detector for every 25 square metres; where high value equipment is installed or the value of the data is high the density should be increased to one detector for every 15 square metres. In unventilated false floors and ceilings there should be not less than one detector for each 20 to 30 square metres, and if the space is divided (for example, by beams) there should be at least one detector in each such space. If the space is ventilated the number of detectors must be increased to give proper protection.

Recommendations are given for tape stores, and other rooms. Every room must have at least one smoke detector. Corridors divided by doors should have one detector in every section, with at least one detector every 12 metres.

Smoke detectors mounted on probes in air-conditioning ducts can give early detection of fire.

Fire detectors should be arranged in zones so that the seat of a fire can be quickly identified with the zone. The zones should be fairly small, with no more than 20 detectors in a zone. The zones should be compatible with the building structure, and its fire compartmentation. The detector zoning should match the air-conditioning zones. Detector zones should not extend across more than one fire compartment. Hidden spaces such as floor voids should form separate zones. Manual call points should be zoned separately from automatic detectors.

The fire-alarm system should have an indicating panel designed to show clearly the location of the origin of the fire alarm. This display should be located outside the computer area in a position agreed with the fire brigade.

The fire-detection system should be tested with a simulated fire to ensure correctness of siting and operation of detectors within the installation. If the detectors are of an approved type their performance can be considered acceptable. The geometry of the area and its furnishings will affect the flow of air. The number of air changes per hour, and the direction of air flow will affect the performance of the fire-detection system. A simulated fire test is essential in large installations. The test fire must not cause corrosion or other damage. Equipment manufacturers should be consulted before any test takes place. BS 6266 describes the two methods of fire simulation in current use, one using a lactose mixture and the other using polyurethane mats. Both methods produce a small controlled fire. Burning polyurethane produces toxic gases, and some people therefore prefer the lactose mixture test.

The fire-detection system should be checked at regular intervals. Special care should be taken to ensure that it is always operative as intended by the designers. Certain zones, or even the entire system, may have to be disabled to allow maintenance or construction work to proceed. The fire authority and the fire insurers should be consulted in such cases. Proper procedures are needed to ensure that the system is fully restored to operation after such events. There should be an independent check.

9 Fire Quenching

PORTABLE EXTINGUISHERS

Hand extinguishers of the carbon dioxide or halon type should be available in easily accessible and visible positions throughout the entire computer facility. Other types of extinguishers should be avoided in computer areas. Extinguishers containing water are dangerous on electrical fires, and dry powder ones produce unacceptable contamination and corrosion.

Water-filled extinguishers of the gas pressure or stored pressure types should be provided near equipment handling large quantities of paper, and in, or immediately outside, rooms or vaults in which records are stored.

There is an FOC list of approved portable fire extinguishers. The appropriate standard is BS 5423, *Specification for Portable Fire Extinguishers*. BSI recently launched the British Approvals for Fire Equipment (BAFE) certification schemes for the manufacture and maintenance of portable extinguishers. Kitemarked extinguishers are available.

Portable fire extinguishers should be coloured coded to show their type at a glance. The standard colour code is:

Red: Water & Carbon dioxide, Soda-acid; suitable for wood, paper, textiles, etc; unsafe at all voltages.

Blue: Dry powder; suitable for flammable liquids, low voltages up to 1000 volts.

Cream: Foam; suitable for flammable liquids; unsafe at all voltages.

Black: Carbon dioxide; suitable for flammable liquids, high voltages.

Green: Vaporising liquids; suitable for flammable liquids, high voltages.

Older extinguishers may not conform to modern colours.

Hose reels, connected to a water supply, should be available in or near to any paper stores.

Adequate access points and space to manoeuvre fire-fighting equipment should be provided both inside and outside the building.

Under no circumstances must water extinguishers be used on live electrical equipment.

All portable fire extinguishers and appliances should be inspected and certified twice each year to ensure that they are fully charged and properly serviceable.

Good quality fire blankets, certified for a range of temperatures, should be fitted in kitchens. They should be visible and be suspended in the supplied container so that the blanket is easily accessible in an emergency. Some cheap glass fibre blankets are not much better than curtain material, and may melt in fires of burning oil or fat.

Computer rooms with modular false floors should have appropriate lifters readily available for use in an emergency.

TRAINING

Few people are trained to make proper use of hand extinguishers. Many people are apprehensive about operating an extinguisher. The instructions printed on the extinguishers are sometimes confusing and may be hard to read. The average person has never handled a fire extinguisher. People are undecided about which way up to hold the extinguisher. Timid people using an extinguisher for the first time may be startled by the force and noise, especially if it is a reasonably big carbon dioxide one. They may simply abandon it, and escape.

At one installation a training session was organised for computer and print room staff. Fire officers from the local brigade demonstrated the finer points of both carbon dioxide and halon BCF extinguishers.

They then invited all the participants to have a go. More than half refused even to take hold of an extinguisher, still less to actually discharge it at a small target.

Fire instructions posted in offices commonly instruct people, when they discover a fire, to "attack the fire with the appropriate extinguisher". Sometimes the instruction is tempered with words of caution, such as "without endangering personal safety". No one should be told to attack a fire without proper training. No one should attack a fire unless there is a second person present. Professional firemen work in pairs. The Fire Precautions Act 1971 states that all persons employed in buildings for which a fire certificate is required should be instructed and trained to ensure that they understand the fire precautions and the action to take in the event of fire.

The literature is full of accounts of people taking extinguishers and going directly away from the fire. One folly is to throw the extinguisher on to the fire! The case of a security guard with leadership qualities is on record. He organised a chain of people to pass extinguishers to him while fighting the blaze before the fire brigade arrived. He threw a total of eighteen extinguishers onto the blaze, one by one. Later he complained bitterly that they not only failed to put out the fire, but that not one of them went off!

Attempting to provide comprehensive fire precautions training for every member of staff may not be feasible. A more effective approach may be to appoint, say, two people in each functional area as "fire wardens", and ensure that they are specifically trained to deal with fire emergencies, and that their training is regularly updated. Other staff would be given more limited training, particularly about how to raise the alarm and what to do when an emergency occurs.

GAS-FLOODING SYSTEMS

Carbon dioxide and certain halon gases are very effective fire-extinguishing agents. (Nitrogen and mixtures of nitrogen and carbon dioxide are also used, but not usually in computer centres.)

Gas-flooding systems are arranged so that in the event of fire the enclosed space can be filled with a sufficient concentration of the extinguishing gas, thus putting out the fire. The gas can reach every nook and cranny of the protected space. Gas flooding is particularly useful for ceiling and floor voids, where it may be impossible to reach a fire using portable hand extinguishers. Gas-flooding systems may introduce the gas through fixed pipework supplied from one or more large storage vessels. Halon systems often use numerous smaller bottles, each with its own nozzle discharging directly into the protected space. Small, compact, self-contained halon systems have been developed recently in which one bottle is connected to a short discharge pipe. The module includes all the necessary control equipment, so that gas-flooding protection is feasible even for small installations.

Halon systems are sometimes used to protect individual cabinets. They may be used to protect electric substations.

The Health and Safety Executive have issued a Guidance Note (GS 16) covering the safety of gas-flooding systems.

The following British Standard publications are relevant:

> BS 5306: Part 4: 1979: Code of Practice for Fire Extinguishing Installations and Equipment on Premises: Carbon Dioxide Systems.
>
> BS 5306: Part 5: Section 1: 1981: Code of Practice for Fire Extinguishing Installations and Equipment on Premises: Halon 1301 Systems.
>
> BS 5306: Part 5: Section 2: Code of Practice for Fire Extinguishing Installations and Equipment on Premises: Halon 1211 Systems (in preparation).

Carbon Dioxide Systems

About thirty per cent concentration of carbon dioxide will extinguish almost any fire in a computer room. Unfortunately carbon dioxide is an asphyxiant gas that is lethal in far lower concentrations than are needed to extinguish a fire, even when there are adequate quantities of oxygen. A concentration of seven per cent leads to stimulation of respiration, and at concentrations over ten per cent the respiratory centre is increasingly depressed. Other symptoms such as headache, visual disturbance, ringing in the ears, and tremor develop, followed by unconsciousness. The concentration of thirty per cent or more used in gas-flooding systems produces immediate asphyxiation.

Deaths have occured in this way.

Any carbon dioxide gas-flooding system must be locked-off whenever staff are present. There must be proper controls to ensure that all persons are accounted for before the gas is discharged, and to prevent re-entry until the gas has been cleared and the area has been properly ventilated. There should be oxygen masks available near areas protected by carbon dioxide systems. The very large volume of gas that must be introduced with carbon dioxide systems may cause damage to equipment by violently dislodging floor or ceiling tiles.

There is very rapid cooling of the air when carbon dioxide is introduced, leading to condensation of moisture on equipment and media. The cooling effect is certain and severe. Often the term "thermal shock" is used to describe it.

Halon Systems

Two halogenated hydrocarbon gases, Halon 1211 and Halon 1301, are commonly used as fire extinguishants, both in gas-flooding systems and portable extinguishers. Halon is short for halogenated hydrocarbon. The halogens are the five chemical elements fluorine, chlorine, bromine, iodine and the rare asatine. Halons are formed by treating hydrocarbon compounds with various halogens. The US Army numbering system is used to designate them. The four digits of the number indicate the relative numbers of the four (or optionally five) different kinds of atoms (carbon, fluorine, chlorine, bromine, and optionally iodine) that form each molecule of the compound.

Halons are effective in much smaller concentrations than carbon dioxide. Typical systems are engineered to give five to eight per cent concentration in the protected spaces.

Halon 1211 (Bromochlorodifluoromethane) or BCF is odourless, and therefore gives no warning of its presence. The Guidance Note suggests that the maximum concentration of BCF in air to which individuals can be exposed for one minute without ill-effects is four to five per cent. This is insufficient for effective fire fighting and below the usual design concentration for BCF systems of five to eight per cent. The toxic effects are stated to include dizziness, impaired co-ordination and reduced mental activity due to the narcotic action of BCF. These effects could impair escape. There may be risk of cardiac arrhythmias (irregularities of the heartbeat), especially where adrenalin levels are raised, as is likely in an emergency. People should never be exposed to BCF at the levels needed for fire fighting.

Halon 1301 (Bromotrifluoromethane) is also known as BTM or sometimes as Pyroforane 1301. It is slightly safer and less toxic than Halon 1211. Halon 1301 is most commonly used in protecting computer rooms, and is much to be preferred to the other two gases, because it is inherently safer. However, it has no smell and gives no warning of its presence, though at concentrations above five or seven per cent it may cause irritation of the eyes. The Guidance Note suggests that short term exposure to a concentration of six per cent or less of Halon 1301 is unlikely to produce undue effects in humans. Concentrations above ten per cent might produce marked disturbances to the central nervous system. Judgement and speed of reaction might be impaired. Unnecessary exposure should be avoided.

Both of the gases may break down in a fire to produce acidic decomposition products, which following acute exposure could cause pulmonary oedema resulting in serious difficulty in breathing. These decomposition products are unlikely to be good for the equipment. The gas must be applied early in the development of the fire to minimise the generation of decomposition products. There should be adequate means for ventilating the space to remove the gas once the fire has been extinguished. The gases are heavier than air, and disposal arrangements need care to avoid subsequent dangers from settlement of the gas in pockets, or in underfloor voids.

Halon gas is expensive, but the cost of discharging it can be much less than the likely loss from an uncontrolled fire in a computer room. Although carbon dioxide is much cheaper than the halon gases, a much greater concentration is needed. The relative costs of extinguishant per cubic metre are about 1:1.06:1.12 for carbon dioxide:Halon 1211:Halon 1301, based on 1984 prices per kilo for the three gases of £1.15, £3.75 and £4.50 respectively. Thus the safest gas, Halon 1301, costs only twelve per cent more than carbon dioxide.

Manual controls to activate the gas discharge when the system is not on automatic are usually provided. For maintenance purposes, means to lock-off the system are also provided.

Approved warning signs must be displayed at each entry point where a total flooding system is in use. Where appropriate, the signs should indicate whether the system is set in automatic or manual mode. There should be an alarm, distinguishable from the fire alarm, and audible in each space protected by the gas-flooding system to give warning of release of the gas. A continuous warning should be displayed at each entry until the atmosphere has been certified safe for re-entry.

Total flooding systems using carbon dioxide and Halon 1211 must be designed to ensure that persons are never present in the protected space during discharge of these agents. They must never be on automatic when people are present, since a fire or a system fault could cause discharge of the gas. Today most computer installations prefer to use Halon 1301.

Paragraphs 32 and 35 of the Guidance Note from the Health and Safety Executive cover the automatic mode of operation for total flooding systems protecting occupied areas using Halon 1301. Automatic mode is permitted in normal circumstances (except during periods of system maintenance) provided certain conditions are met. The achieved concentration in air after discharge should be six per cent or less by volume. The system should not operate unless signals are received from separate fire-detectoin systems. There should be a time delay after sounding the alarm to allow persons to escape. The Guidance Note suggests that 30 seconds should be sufficient. There should be a "panic button" inside the protected space, which while pressed will prevent the release of the gas. BS 5306, dealing with the design of Halon 1301 systems, specifies a maximum delay of 30 seconds, and requires a substantial discharge within 10 seconds.

People working near a protected space should be adequately trained in the action to be taken in the event of discharge, and a suitable emergency procedure should be established. The discharge is very noisy and, if not experienced before, it could be a little frightening. Some firms of fire engineers have film and video material that can be used to train personnel.

SPRINKLERS

Water-sprinkler systems were first used to protect cotton mills in 1866.

They are widely used in the United States. Sprinklers are normally very much slower to operate than any other form of fire protection, and so they are an excellent long stop. A large fire is needed to cause a sprinkler system to operate, and sprinklers can be on all the time but are very slow to respond, and not prone to false alarms.

Historically it has not been considered desirable to have a sprinkler system within a computer suite. Sprinklers may leak, or may be set off by accident if the head or the pipework are damaged, possibly by frost. This is unlikely to happen within a computer suite. However, pre-action systems are available, in which the water is kept in check, clear of the sprinkler heads, until warning of fire has been given by heat or smoke detectors. There may be impurities in the water from a conventional sprinkler system which could damage electronic equipment. Clean water systems are coming into use. These use previously uncharged clean lines to feed clean water to the discharge points. They use sensitive detectors, and delayed discharge, that allow human intervention so that false alarms and minor fires can be handled without shutting down the entire installation. Power can be disconnected before discharge occurs. Equipment can be covered in waterproof plastic sheets if there is time.

The sprinkler head operates only when the temperature reaches some high pre-set value indicating that there is a fire directly underneath. The sprinkling in thus localised to the area of the fire. The sprinklers act independently of one another and if the first fails to stop the fire, others will operate.

Water from a sprinkler may fail to reach a fire inside an equipment cabinet. Wet equipment may corrode, unless it is promptly cleaned and dried, preferably by those experienced in such work. The Insurance Technical Bureau has special knowledge of this area.

Thinking in the insurance world is tending to favour use of spinklers as a long stop, when other fire-quenching systems, such as gas flooding, have failed to stem the fire. Sprinkler systems are appropriate for large installations, perhaps with gas-flooding systems as well. Most fires will be controlled by one sprinkler only, but there could be lots of water and smoke damage. The material damage to the building, caused by a fire, might be limited by a sprinkler system to perhaps £50,000, instead of several millions for the whole building.

PLANT AND AUXILIARY EQUIPMENT

Large computer centres will have plant rooms, electric substations, and other auxiliaries that demand proper fire protection. Foam systems are often used in such areas.

It is essential to arrange for cut-off of oil and gas supplies in the event of a fire incident.

10 Operational Aspects

INTRODUCTION

Design of a modern computer installation usually includes careful consideration of fire precautions and other security needs. There is good structural fire protection, and effective fire-detection and fire-quenching systems are installed. A well-designed installation may still be vulnerable unless it has adequate operational fire precautions. Management attitude determines the effectiveness of operational fire precautions. As the code of practice BS 6266 says, "there is no substitute for determined and disciplined attitudes and action in relation to housekeeping, general tidiness and control of combustibles within the EDP area". Without management support, the defences will be eroded, and the installation will be exposed to unnecessary risk.

STAFF RESPONSIBILITIES

Staff responsibilities must be clearly defined. A senior member of staff should be responsible for the operational fire precautions in the whole computer area. Procedures should be established and monitored to ensure that fire precautions are included as an essential part of normal working practice.

Operations staff often work in small groups of two or three at night. They lack the support of colleagues that daytime workers enjoy. Some managements still allow one person to operate a computer alone in an empty building at night or during the weekend. Quite apart from the asset security implications, the situation might be a disaster for the individual concerned. Allowing one person to work alone may contravene the Health and Safety at Work, etc Act 1974, unless there are adequate formal means for regular checking on the safety of the individual concerned, as for instance by security guards checking not less frequently than once each hour. As well as the fire risks there is danger from machinery, and the potential for fatal electric shock. Armed robbers have attacked and injured computer staff working alone out-of-hours.

TRAINING

Under Section 2 of the Health and Safety at Work Act it is the responsibility of employers to provide such information, instruction and supervision as is necessary to ensure, so far as is reasonably practicable, the health and safety at work of the employees.

The Home Office Guide to the Fire Precautions Act 1971 states, "all persons employed in buildings for which a fire certificate is required should be instructed and trained to ensure that they understand the fire precautions and action to take in the event of fire". Mere *instruction* is not sufficient, the staff must be *trained*.

Staff should be trained in the fire regulations applicable to their place of work, in the procedures for dealing with fires, and in the use of hand extinguishers. There should be periodic fire exercises, to ensure that the procedures are understood, and that they are likely to work. There should be a continuous fire precaution and control campaign, to increase awareness and understanding.

Once the staff become involved in regular fire precautions training they are much more likely to accept the need for a systematic programme of daily checks as part of normal work. Attitude is vital.

EVACUATION

In a fire emergency the aim is to permit everyone to reach safety in less than two and a half minutes. The importance of this time is based on tests on fires involving plastics, especially polyurethane and PVC, which reach maximum severity in a few minutes. After this time, due to the heat and toxicity of the dense black smoke produced, it is virtually impossible for anyone to escape from affected areas without injury.

The importance of prompt evacuation must be stressed. Special arrangements must be made to cater for disabled people, who may need assistance during an evacuation.

The Home Office *Guides to the Fire Precautions Act 1971. Number 3. Offices, Shops and Railway Premises* gives rules for escape routes and travelling distance, as explained in Chapter 3.

As mentioned earlier, people tend to go out of any building by the route they used to enter it. They retrace their steps. Fire instructions should ensure that the correct routes are known and clearly signposted. Training drills should be used to check that people do know and use the appropriate emergency escape routes, and not go the wrong, long way round.

Fire exits and corridors are frequently obstructed by stores of various kinds. This should not be tolerated. All gangways, passages and staircases must be kept free from any obstruction whatever.

Exit routes should be clearly signposted with approved green rectangular safety signs, showing clearly the correct directions. All signs should conform to the *Safety Signs Regulations 1980,* which are mandatory, even for existing signs, from 1 January 1986.

All exit routes should be fitted with automatic emergency lighting, which should be regularly tested to ensure its continued efficiency. Dead ends, such as store rooms, should be kept locked, and should be clearly labelled.

Escape routes are often protected by a number of self-closing fire check doors at intervals along corridors, and at staircase landings. The doors are arranged in such a way as to prevent any spread of smoke and fumes along corridors and up stairways. Without this protection alternate escape routes may become impassable. Moreover the fire itself may spread very rapidly to all parts of a building if the doors are not shut. All such doors should be clearly labelled on both faces at about eye height with the words "Fire door – keep shut". Such fire check doors are often found wedged open, so that they are quite useless. Management should never permit this, and those responsible should be disciplined. A much better arrangement is to have self-closing doors as described in Chapter 3, normally latched open by an electromagnet linked to the fire-detection system.

Emergency exit doors to the outside should be checked regularly to ensure that the release mechanism operates correctly. Panic latches or panic bolts, if properly maintained, are probably safer than either glass bolts or keys in glass-fronted boxes. Such doors should have the words "Push bar to open" in conspicuous lettering immediately above the bar. Doors can be protected by an alarm circuit to ensure that they are not used without authorisation, and that they are not left open by accident. This may be important if the door opens on to a public street. Such exits are often obstructed by thoughtless passers-by. They should be labelled conspicuously on the outside face at about eye level with the words "Fire exit – keep clear". Any obstructions should be removed without delay.

Normally lifts must never be used during a fire emergency. The lift shaft might act as a flue for rising smoke, fumes and heat. The lift itself might become stopped between floors, if the power failed. Personnel could become trapped in an inaccessible situation, from which rescue would be difficult. However, in some very tall buildings special emergency lifts are installed and designated for the purpose.

Special care is needed where turnstiles or revolving doors are installed. Usually emergency escape doors will be fitted alongside. There must always be free passage for emergencies. Powered turnstiles should not be used as part of an escape route.

Where an automatic access control system is installed, special care must be taken to ensure that free passage is permitted in emergency. Usually controlled doors are latched by an electric strike. This is arranged so that power locks the door, and it is released by dropping the power. In the event of a fire alarm , the doors can be released by dropping the power to each electric strike, so that the system can be made fail safe.

Very great care is needed to ensure that those spaces protected by gas-quenching systems have foolproof escape routes under all conditions.

Fire assembly points should be designated for all personnel. Assembly points should be clearly marked. All staff should be told which assembly point they should report to. The assembly points should be well clear of the building, in positions that are not likely to hinder the emergency services when they arrive. The positions selected should so far as possible be free from danger from falling glass and debris, and should take account of the possible dangers that might follow upon a bomb attack.

Lists of personnel should be available to the senior officer, so that a speedy check can be made to account for all those persons who might be involved. Reception or security staff should have lists of those staff who are known to be absent, and also the names of any visitors or contractors. Various systems exist to facilitate checking the roll for missing persons. Automatic time and attendance systems may help. Traditional attendance registers and visitors' books are good for reasonable numbers, provided that they are properly supervised at all times. They are quite useless in a fire situation if the record is not a reliable and accurate record of those who are present on site at the time. Another technique is to post a daily list of staff plus visitors within every geographical section, and require everyone to sign in and out as a matter of course. If there is an incident the appointed "fire warden" for the section, or his alternate, then checks the list, and accounts for everyone before reporting to the senior responsible officer.

ACTION IN CASE OF FIRE

Fire instructions and planning should emphasise that personal safety is the most important consideration. (The most expensive installation can be rebuilt in time, but a life is irreplaceable.)

Clear instructions about the action to be taken in case of fire should be worked out and displayed at appropriate points throughout the computer area.

In the largest installations the emergency action will be the province of security and engineering personnel, rather then computer operations staff.

The emergency instructions should be taught to all staff and personnel who have access to the computer area. The operators' console should have a copy of the instructions to hand at all times, together with any temporary special instructions.

The points to be covered in the instructions will include: the importance and urgency of raising the alarm, and the means for doing so; the procedure for notifying the fire brigade; evacuating personnel and ensuring that the building is clear, with details of the assembly points, and method of calling the roll; notifying senior key personnel; the method for shutting down the installation; the location of the emergency controls used to isolate the equipment from the power supplies and for closing down the air conditioning system, and the circumstances under which this should be done; the means for attempting to extinguish a small fire using portable appliances without exposing personnel to danger; and the means for releasing a gas-flooding system once personnel are clear, and the conditions under which this should be done.

GENERAL HOUSEKEEPING

All waste should be cleared away at the end of the working period, and not less frequently than once each day. Waste should be stored securely until collected so that it cannot be ignited by vandals.

Lint from paper, particularly from bursting operations, ignites easily and burns very rapidly. The space under a raised floor collects lint and should be cleared regularly unless it is used as a forced air plenum with proper filtration. There should be sufficient clearance below the floor to permit easy cleaning, even beneath areas occupied be equipment. At least six to eight inches will be necessary. The equipment supplier should be consulted.

Frequent checks should be made throughout the installation to minimise the quantities of combustible materials of any kind. Flammable cleaning fluids should have a flash point greater than 65 degrees C, and should not be kept within the computer area.

Store rooms, plant rooms, and access doors to fire stacks, ducts, and false ceilings should be kept locked at all times to prevent unauthorised access. Correctly labelled keys for all doors should be available within the secure area, preferably on a key board, marked to match.

Plant rooms should be kept clean and tidy. They should not be used to store rubbish, spare equipment and plant, or contractors' and maintenance supplies. Floor and ceiling voids should be inspected regularly to ensure that they are free from dust and combustible materials.

CONTRACTORS

Building work and maintenance tend to introduce special threats of fire into a building. Paint stripping and welding are obviously hazardous activities. Adhesives and special solvents may introduce unexpected risks. All building maintenance and construction work should be monitored to ensure that no uncontrolled hazards are introduced. The work should be inspected to ensure that existing precautions, such as fire stopping, are correctly reinstated.

Electrical repairs and alterations should satisfy the highest electrical engineering standards. Maintenance work on the electrical installation or air-conditioning system may require that the fire-alarm system has to be disabled, either partly or completely. This situation needs vigilance, especially to ensure that the system is correctly restored to full operation. Where a gas-flooding system is installed there is a danger that the gas might be released by accident when the system is restored. Due care should be exercised to ensure that this cannot happen.

The Fire Authority may have to be informed if the work has a material impact upon the fire precautions, even if this impact is only temporary.

SMOKING, FOOD AND REST AREAS

There must be a clear policy on smoking. Smoking will be prohibited throughout the computer area, including in machine rooms, media libraries, and plant rooms.

Standard signs should be prominently displayed in areas where smoking is prohibited. In areas where it is permitted, ashtrays or sandbins should be provided, and emptied regularly. A legitimate time and place for smoking should be provided; whatever the rules, some smokers will smoke. If it is not officially allowed they will still do it in storerooms, and other risky places.

Food and drink should be confined to rest areas, because coffee and cigarettes tend to go hand in hand. Spillages of drinks may cause serious damage to media and electronic equipment, with risk of fire. Drinks and food should never be permitted near terminals, keyboards or printers, or in equipment rooms and media libraries.

Portable heaters should not be permitted in rest areas.

Steel lockers should be used for outdoor clothing and personal effects.

END-OF-WORK PROCEDURES

An installation is perhaps most vulnerable to the threat from fire when it is left unoccupied. Nobody is there to see or smell trouble. Many smaller installations have no form of automatic fire-detection system. Smaller sites tend to work regular office hours, so they are exposed to the danger of an undetected outbreak 75 per cent of the time.

End-of-work procedures are an essential part of the fire precautions for every installation. There should be a defined routine for closing down the system at the end of the working day.

Normally all electrical equipment should be unplugged from the wall sockets. However, the suppliers may recommend that certain equipment should be left connected to the mains power, to avoid problems of power surges and thermal shock at switch-on. Some equipment may be needed for unattended out-of-hours operations. This typically applies to some communications equipment. One useful idea is to mark or colour-code the plugs of such equipment, so that security staff know that the equipment should not be disconnected.

The installation should be powered down in accordance with the manufacturer's instructions. Kitchens and rest areas should be checked to ensure that cookers and kettles are switched off at the mains and unplugged wherever possible, and that ashtrays are safe.

All waste should be removed from the computer area. Media should be returned to secure storage after taking final dumps and back-up copies. Procedures should be specified for securing other vital manual records.

All hatches and doors should be secured. Master switches will be turned to OFF. The fire-alarm system may have to be set to call the brigade automatically, either by a direct link to a calling station or by an auto-dialling telephone link. Gas-flooding systems will be set to automatic once personnel are clear of the protected areas.

If any special maintenance or building work is in progress special written instructions should be given that the areas that might be affected shall be inspected.

The senior person on duty should check the entire computer suite before the premises are secured. Any intruder alarm must be set to active. Final locking of doors, and the method for handover of the keys should be clearly specified. The senior person, and perhaps all the staff, might be required to sign a timed logbook, before a departure from the site.

Where security personnel are on watch outside normal hours, they should visit the computer areas periodically as part of their patrols. This should be done, as an additional safeguard, even where the computer staff are operating the system.

On sites without out-of-hours security staff, consideration should be given to appointing a reputable key holder, known to the police, so that access is possible in an emergency.

11 Guidelines

PRECAUTIONS

1. Ensure that the building, and any proposed extension or alteration to it, complies with the relevant building regulations.
2. Ensure that the computer facility has a valid fire certificate where one is required.
3. Check that any proposed alterations to the premises or its uses would not invalidate any fire certificate.
4. Consult the fire insurers about any proposed changes that might affect the fire precautions of the premises.
5. Seek expert advice from the local fire service, and maintain good liaison with them.
6. Obtain the computer equipment manufacturer's recommendations about fire precautions, and take account of them.
7. Ensure that the installation and its procedures comply with the requirements of the Health and Safety at Work Act 1974 and of the Health and Safety Executive.
8. Ensure that the installation is remote from any possible hazard from nearby industrial processes or stores of dangerous materials.
9. Avoid having stores of fuel nearby, eg for heating or for vehicles.

10. Eliminate risks of explosion that might arise from underground leakage of town gas or sewer gas into the subfloors or basements.

11. Ensure that vehicles carrying hazardous or highly flammable loads cannot approach the building.

THE BUILDING

12. Wherever possible, house the computer operation in a separate building of non-combustible construction reserved solely for the purpose.

13. In shared premises, ensure that the computer area is separated from all other activities by imperforate and waterproof walls, floors and ceilings, all having a fire-resistance time appropriate for the fire load associated with the activities in the neighbouring areas.

14. Eliminate and stop-up all openings in these walls, floors and ceilings that are not essential for operational or safety reasons

15. Ensure that every essential opening in the walls, floors or ceilings that are not essential for operational or safety reasons. that conform to the Fire Offices' Committee's *Rules for the Construction and Installation of Fire Break Doors, Lobbies and Shutters.*

16. Avoid having windows that might be exposed to external fires.

17. Ensure that all essential windows are vandal resistant, and preferably of wired-glass in metal frames.

18. Ensure that flood water from the fire fighting or other activities cannot accidentally enter the computer area. If possible ensure that its floor is at a higher level then the surrounding areas, or that all doorways are protected by raised sills, with ramps where appropriate

19. Ensure that underfloor voids have drainage channels, and waterways to clear any possible flooding. Fit pumps if necessary.

20. Keep an adequate supply of clean, large, waterproof plastic

sheets available in the computer area. These may be used to cover equipment so as to prevent the ingress of water from roof leaks or flooding on a higher floor.

21. Keep supplies of dust-free non-toxic absorbent materials available to cope with minor spillages.

22. Wherever possible ensure that services and ventilation ducts for other areas do not pass through the computer area. Where such ducts must pass through the computer area, construct them as fire-resisting shafts.

23. Ensure that any ventilation and service ducts that serve the computer area do not pass through other areas. Where they must do so, construct them as fire-resisting shafts.

24. Ensure that all ancilliary areas are separated from the main equipment areas by fire-resistant walls from true floor to true ceiling.

25. If possible divide large rooms into smaller ones by fire-resistant screens from true floor to true ceiling.

26. Ensure that raised floors are supported on non-combustible materials of adequate strength, and that the floor is made from fire-resisting materials, or clad with such materials on the underside.

27. Ensure that all materials used to line walls, ceilings, and ducts are non-combustible and that they do not give rise to dust or to toxic or corrosive fumes when heated.

28. Avoid bringing water, steam and gas service pipes into the computer area.

29. Ensure that all holes provided for cables and services in the fire-resisting walls are properly fire-stopped to prevent ingress of smoke, fumes, heat or water. Inspect such fire stopping periodically, and after any alterations or maintenance, to ensure that its integrity has not been compromised.

30. Inspect and clean floor and ceiling voids regularly.

31. Monitor all building work and maintenance to ensure that no uncontrolled hazards are created.

32. Inform the Fire Authority if the work is likely to have a material impact on the fire precautions even if this is only temporary.

ELECTRIC POWER

33. Ensure that all electrical installation work complies with the current edition of the *Regulations for the Electrical Equipment of Buildings* issued by the Institution of Electrical Engineers. All work should be carried out to the highest standards.

34. Consider possible alternate sources of power to replace the public supply, and take appropriate action.

35. Ensure that all standby generators, motor alternator sets, and oil-filled electrical equipment are installed remote from the computer area, and safe against attack.

36. Ensure that fire-retardant cables are used throughout the installation, and that underfloor cables are of the steel armoured type. Consider using cables insulated with materials that do not contain halogens, sulphur or nitrogen.

37. Have a sufficient number of switched pocket outlets, each with indicator lamps, arranged in convenient positions, to reduce the need to use extension leads for test equipment or cleaning machines.

38. Do not have underfloor socket outlets.

39. Provide emergency knock-off controls for the power supply and for the air conditioning near to the main console, and adjacent to the main exit doors from the computer area. Ensure that these emergency switches are clearly labelled, and shrouded or otherwise protected to guard against accidental operation.

40. Provide suitable automatic emergency lighting to ensure that all safety exit routes are illuminated even if the main power should fail. Keep a large torch or lantern at the main operators' console.

41. Provide a main isolator switch for use by the fire brigade, controlling all power supplies except those to lighting and

smoke extraction. This switch should be labelled FIRE EMERGENCY ELECTRICAL ISOLATION SWITCH, and may be protected by a glass-fronted box.

AIR CONDITIONING AND SERVICES

42. Ensure that the air-conditioning system is entirely separate from any other system.

43. Ensure that the operation of the fire alarm shuts down the air-conditioning system.

44. Ensure that all ducts are fitted with automatic fire-shutters or dampers where they pass through fire segregation walls, floors or ceilings. The dampers should be operated by smoke detectors, and have easy manual means for both closing and resetting them.

45. Provide adequate means for removing smoke from the computer area, but ensure that operation of the smoke-extraction system cannot reduce the air pressure in the computer area and so induct smoke from elsewhere. Manual controls for the smoke-extraction system should be located outside the computer area, and be suitably labelled and protected against unauthorised operation.

46. Check that air filters are made of non-combustible materials, and that they are cleaned regularly to remove lint and other combustible materials.

47. Check that all plant is maintained correctly in accordance with the manufacturer's schedules, and that it is properly lubricated and adjusted to compensate for wear. Ensure that plant rooms are kept clean and free from waste.

48. Where unit air conditioners are used, check that they are fitted with themal cut-outs and alarms to monitor overheating of bearings or motors, failure of fans, blockage of filters, or water leakage.

49. Check that any header tanks for heating and air-conditioning systems are so sited that leakage or overflow cannot cause flooding of the computer room. Ensure that valve washers are replaced from time to time. Protect such tanks from frost

in winter.

50. Where supplementary heaters are installed to protect equipment against failure of air conditioning in winter, ensure that they cannot become obstructed.

51. Provide emergency shut-off controls for gas and water supplies.

CONTENTS

52. Ensure that decorative finishes, furniture and fittings are made from fire-resistant materials. Ensure that all soft furnishings are flame retardant.

53. Provide steel bins for waste, fitted with self-closing lids. Ensure that waste is removed frequently and stored securely awaiting collection.

54. Have no more stationery within the computer area than is essential for immediate use. Keep such supplies neatly boxed, with no loose sheets.

55. Hold main supplies of stationery away from the computer area in locked storerooms.

56. Ensure that printout, cards, paper tape, ribbons, and all other combustible materials are not left about loose. Shredded and de-collated paper is highly combustible, and should be kept in fire resistant containers to be removed from the building without delay. Waste should be tightly baled to reduce the fire risk.

57. Keep all cleaning materials and engineers' supplies in closed metal cabinets, with no more stock than is needed for immediate use.

58. Provide steel lockers for outdoor clothing and personal effects.

59. Ensure that cooking facilities do not introduce unnecessary hazards.

VITAL RECORDS

60. Have suitable data safes or fire- and moisture-proof vaults

to protect essential records and media.

61. Arrange suitable secure off-site storage for back-up media and other essential supplies.

62. Arrange suitable schedules and procedures to ensure correct movement of media between the several stores, and correct rotation of supplies.

63. Produce current lists of vital files, showing the identity of the storage media, and the location of each of the several copies. Deposit copies of these lists at each store, and monitor the actual contents against the lists to ensure that the back-up procedures are working correctly.

64. Take professional advice about the most suitable location for a data safe.

65. Keep the doors of data safes closed unless media is actually being inserted or removed.

66. Ensure that all essential documentation is properly safeguarded against loss by fire.

FIRE DETECTION

67. Install an automatic fire-detection system linked to alarms to protect the entire computer area, with adequate numbers of temperature detectors and smoke detectors of appropriate types in all enclosed spaces.

68. Have manual alarm points at strategic positions.

69. Have accurate and up-to-date floor plans available at a suitable control point outside the computer area, so that they may be available to the senior fire officer at an incident. The floor plan should be posted next to the panel which identifies the smoke or fire detector that has been triggered.

70. Ensure that the fire alarm is linked to a building security guard post and/or directly to the Fire Service or other external emergency call service.

71. Ensure that the fire-alarm signal is audible throughout the installation taking account of the normal high levels of

background noise.

72. Mark the positions of all underfloor smoke/fire/water detectors on the floor panels that cover them. Either ensure that equipment does not obscure these markings, or else mark adjacent panels.

FIRE QUENCHING

73. Provide appropriate types of portable extinguishers for dealing with electrical, paper, and other types of fire, prominently placed at strategic locations throughout the installation. Ensure that all appliances conform to appropriate standards. Have them inspected and certified at regular intervals, and recharged if necessary.

74. Manual fire extinguishers should be capable of being operated by all employees.

75. Train all personnel in the correct handling and use of fire-fighting equipment.

76. Where modular floors are used have the correct kind of lifter available and accessible, in a well-marked position, and reserved for emergency use.

77. Fire-resistant and waterproof covers may be made available to protect equipment in case there is sufficient time to use them before fire gets hold.

78. Where gas-flooding systems are used, ensure that the installation and its operation comply with the Guidance Note issued by the Health and Safety Executive.

79. Ensure that any gas-flooding system protects all parts of the installation, including floor voids and false ceilings. Have it checked regularly.

80. Where a fire-extinguishing system requires an electric power supply, provide a suitable standby, otherwise a combination of mains failure and fire could be catastrophic.

81. Consider using a sprinkler system in a large installation, especially one of the clean water type. Provide a shut-off valve

accessible to authorised personnel.

82. In remote areas ensure that an emergency supply of water is available reserved for fire-fighting purposes.

PERSONNEL AND EVACUATION

83. Define staff responsibilities clearly in writing.

84. Post clear instructions about the action to be taken in case of fire, and ensure that all personnel understand them.

85. Conduct fire drills at reasonable intervals, and ensure that the building can be cleared completely in less than two and a half minutes.

86. Test audible alarms regularly. Ensure that everywhere in the premises such alarms can be heard clearly above the normal background noises.

87. Establish a sound and speedy procedure to ensure that all persons, including visitors and temporary workers, can be accounted for in an emergency.

88. Ensure that all escape routes are correctly signed, and that they are kept free from any obstruction. All signs should conform to the Safety Signs Regulations 1980, and comply with BS 5378: Part 1: 1980. Consider using luminous signs.

89. Check regularly that all emergency exit doors operate freely from the inside. Fit alarms to all emergency exits to prevent unauthorised use, especially to admit a collaborator from the outside.

90. Prohibit the wedging of fire check doors, and class it as a disciplinary offence.

91. Ensure that all doors to storerooms, plant rooms, fire stacks, ducts, and false ceilings are appropriately marked and are kept locked. Provide a labelled keyboard within the secure area, complete with labelled keys for each such door.

92. Prohibit smoking throughout the computer area, and display "No Smoking" signs. Provide a rest area where smoking is permitted, and have sand bins or deep non-combustible

ashtrays that are regularly cleared in a safe manner.

93. Prohibit food and drink in the computer area and media libraries, and in the vicinity of any terminals, printers or keyboards.

94. Devise appropriate procedures for the actions to be taken at the end of any period of work, and monitor to ensure that they are followed.

95. Consider using a reputable key-holding service, known to the police, where the premises are unoccupied out of hours.

Useful Addresses

British Standards Institution
2 Park Street
London W1A 2BS — 01-629 9000
Telex 266933

or

Lynford Wood
Milton Keynes
MK14 6LE — 0908-320033

Computer Security Institute
43 Boston Post Road
Northborough
Massachusetts
MA 01532
USA

Fire Insurers' Research and Testing Organisation
Melrose Avenue
Borehamwood
Hertfordshire
WD6 2BJ — 01-207 2345

Fire Offices' Commitee
Aldermary House
Queen Street
London EC4N 1TT — 01-248 4477

Fire Protection Association
140 Aldersgate Street
London EC1A 4HX 01-606 3757

Fire Research Station
Building Research Establishment
Borehamwood
Hertfordshire
WD6 2BL 01-953 6177
Telex 8951648

Health and Safety Executive
Baynards House
1 Chepstow Place
London W2 4TF

Home Office Fire Department
Queen Anne's Gate
London SW1

Institution of Fire Engineers
148 New Walk
Leicester
LE1 7QB 0533-59171

Insurance Technical Bureau
52 Grosvenor Gardens
London SW1W 0AU 01-730 8847/8948

National Computing Centre Limited
Oxford Road
Manchester M1 7ED 061-228 6333

Further Reading

JOURNALS AND DIRECTORIES

Computer Security Journal, (Two to three issues a year), Computer Security Institute

Computers and Security, North Holland

Fire, (Monthly), Unisaf Publications, Queensway House, 2 Queensway, Redhill, Surrey RH1 1QS, 0737-68611

Fire International, (Bi-Monthly), Unisaf Publications

Fire Prevention, (Ten times a year), Fire Protection Association

Fire Protection, (Monthly), A E Morgan Publications, Stanley House West Street, Epsom, Surrey KT18 7RL

Fire Protection Directory, (Annual), A E Morgan Publications

Fire Surveyor, Victor Green Publications, Cavendish House, 128-134 Cleveland Street, London W1ZP 5DN, 01-387 5050

Health and Safety at Work, Maclaren Publishers Ltd, Davis House, 69-77 High Street, Croyden CR9 1QH, 01-688 7788

Institution of Fire Engineers Quarterly

International Security Directory, Court & Judicial Publishing Company Ltd

International Security Review, (Bi-Monthly), Unisaf Publications

Risk and Loss Management, (Monthly), United Trade Press Ltd, UTP House, 33-35 Bowling Green Lane, London EC1R 0DA

Security and Fire Protection Yearbook, Victor Green Publications

Security Gazette, 109-119 Waterloo Road, London SE1 8LU, 01-928 3388

Security and Protection, (Monthly), Batiste Publications, Pembroke House, Campsbourne Road, London N8 7BR, 01-340 3291

The Yellow Book, Unisaf Publications

OTHER PUBLICATIONS

Annual Report for 1984, Fire Protection Association

Attacking the Fire Menace, BSI News, January 1985, p 14
(Gives details of the launch of the British Approvals for Fire Equipment (BAFE) scheme and kitemarking for portable fire extinguishers)

Barclay S, *Fire*, Hamish Hamilton, 1972
(Gives a very readable layman's account of fire disasters around the world, including several in the UK)

Beckingham H, *The Law and the Use of Fire Extinguishers,* Health and Safety at Work, May 1981, pp 37-38

British Standard code of practice for *Fire Protection for Electronic Data Processing Installations,* BS 6266: 1982, BSI
(The definitive work, but written for specialists)

Building Contents Analysed, Fire International, February 1985, pp 73-76
(Gives much information about the behaviour of furnishing materials in fire conditions)

Chadwick H A, *Burning Down the Data Centre,* Datamation, October 1975

Code of Practice: Means of Escape in Case of Fire, Greater London Council, Publication 7168 14382, Reprinted July 1984

Compendium of Fire Safety Data, Six Volumes, Fire Protection Association
(Comprises more than 245 data sheets on all aspects of fire, its prevention and control. Further sheets are produced each year. Volumes of special interest in the context of fire protection of

computer systems include: 1 Organisation and fire safety:management of fire risks; 3 Housekeeping and general fire precautions, nature and behaviour of fire; 5 Fire protection equipment and systems; 6 Buildings and fire)

Computer Security Handbook, Computer Security Institute, 43 Boston Post Road, Northborough, MA 01532, USA
(Contains reprints, mainly of US origin, of significant papers and articles on all aspects of computer security, including fire protection and contingency planning. Bibliography)

Connor S, *Carbon Monoxide – the Unknown Gas,* Fire International, June 1984, pp 41-43
(Gives much information about the effects of carbon monoxide and the treatment of those affected)

Duffy N M, *Countdown Services: Fire and its Aftermath in a Computer Bureau,* Information and Management, Volume 3, Number 3, September 1980, North Holland

Fire in Buildings, Health and Safety at Work, December 1981, pp 14-17

Fire Directory 1984/85 (Yellow Book), Unisaf Publications
(A comprehensive guide to the public and industrial fire brigades, associations, and fire protection manufacturers)

Fire Precautions Log, Croner Publications Ltd, Croner House, 173 Kingston Road, New Maldon, Surrey KT3 3SS, 01-942 8966
(Designed for those charged with day-to-day operation of fire-precautions systems at individual locations, it offers general advice on fire precautions. It includes sections to record routine action, checks and maintenance in areas like staff training, means of escape, fire-fighting equipment and alarm systems, automatic detection, fire doors, emergency lighting, water-sprinkler installations)

Fire Precautions Register, Croner Publications Ltd
(Designed for use by anyone with overall responsibility for the maintenance and safety of premises. Covers the essential background to the legislation as well as the requirements and conditions of fire certificates. It includes the Fire Precautions Log)

FITECH International, Unisaf International
(This is an annual catalogue of some of the fire-fighting and fire-protection equipment that is available)

Gas-Flooding Fire-Extinguishing Systems: Toxic Hazards and Precautions, Guidance Note GS 16, Health and Safety Executive, August 1982, HMSO (ISBN 0 11 883548 3)
(Essential reading for all those involved in any aspect of gas-flooding systems)

Heels R, *The Design of Gaseous Extinguishing Systems,* Fire Protection, April 1985, pp 14-15

Home Office *Guides to the Fire Precautions Act 1971. Number 3. Offices, Shops and Railway Premises,* HMSO, 1977 (ISBN 0 11 340445 X); Fourth impression (with two amendments), 1984

Home Office Manual of Firemanship, *Book 8, Building Construction and Fire Protection,* HMSO, 1977 (ISBN 0 11 340588 X); *Book 9, Fire Protection of Buildings,* HMSO, 1977 (ISBN 0 11 340589 8)

National Fire Prevention and Control Administration, *Standard Practice for the Fire Protection of Essential Electronic Equipment,* US Department of Commerce RP-1, 1978
(Contains details of many actual fires in computer and similar electronic installations)

Perkins C, *Fire Losses Involving Electronic Equipment – The Importance of Preventing Corrosion,* Policy, June 1976, p 472

Read R E H and Morris W A, *Aspects of Fire Precautions in Buildings,* HMSO, 1982 (ISBN 0 11 671355 0)
(Gives guidance on the structural aspects of fire protection in buildings, and an account of the current legislation in the UK. It includes an appendix listing regulations, codes of practice, and standards)

Recommendations for the Protection of Computer Installations against Fire, Fire Offices' Committee, December 1979
(This gives detailed recommendations for the construction, equipment and space protection of installations. Air-conditioning systems and protection of records are covered, and there are specifications for halon and carbon dioxide flooding systems)

Schroeder P, *Every Mishap Costs Money,* Risk and Loss Management, January 1985, pp 6-10

Spotlight on Cables, Fire International 91, February-March 1985, pp 47-51

(A review of many products designed to minimise the hazards from cables. It includes several cables with low emission of toxic gases)

Squires T, *Computer Security – The Personnel Aspect,* NCC Publications, 1980

(This covers protection from people and protection of people. The effects of the Health and Safety at Work legislation are covered, as well as people in contingency situations)

Taylor J and Cooke G, *The Fire Precautions Act in Practice,* Architectural Press, 1978

The Danger of Unsealed Cable Transits, Fire International, February 1985, pp 35-38

Ward R, *Fire Protection of Computers: Fixed Systems and Software Protection,* Fire Prevention 173, October 1984, pp 27-31

(Discusses the application of gas-flooding and sprinkler systems to computer suites, and provision of fire-protected storage. Gives ten case histories of computer fires in the UK)

Waring L P,*Management Handbook of Computer Security,* Section 2.5, NCC Publications, 1978

(Contains essential guidance on fire precautions in computer installations. Bibliography)

Why Have Non-Halogen Cables?, Fire International 91, February-March 1985, pp 43-46

FILMS, VIDEO AND OTHER MATERIAL

Anatomy of a Fire, Central Film Library, Chalfont Grove, Gerrards Cross, Bucks SL9 8TN

(A film or video about the Fire Research Station investigation of the Dublin disco fire. Illustrates the problems presented by fires in large buildings where there is rapid spread)

Understanding Fire, Fire Protection Association

(The nature of fire, how it starts and spreads, and how it can be controlled. The FPA has seven other films and videos. It also has sets of slides for use in staff training, and posters on fire protection)